WORLD
HISTORY SERIES ■■■

The Roman Republic

by
Don Nardo

Lucent Books, P.O. Box 289011, San Diego, CA 92198-9011

Titles in The World History Series

The Age of Feudalism   The Hundred Years War
Ancient Greece   The Roman Empire
The French and Indian War   The Roman Republic
Hitler's Reich   The Russian Revolution

Library of Congress Cataloging-in-Publication Data

Nardo, Don, 1947–
    The Roman Republic / by Don Nardo.
        p.   cm.—(World history series)
    Includes bibliographical references and index.
    Summary: Traces the history of the Roman Republic from
the founding of Rome through its wars, conquests, and expansion to the fall of the Republic.
    ISBN 1-56006-230-4
    1. Rome—History—Republic, 510–30 B.C.—Juvenile litera-
ture. [1. Rome—History—Republic, 510–30 B.C.]
    I. Title.   II. Series.
DG231.7.N37   1994
937'.02—dc20   93-6905
                                                    CIP
                                                     AC

Contents

Foreword

Each year on the first day of school, nearly every history teacher faces the task of explaining why his or her students should study history. One logical answer to this question is that exploring what happened in our past explains how the things we often take for granted—our customs, ideas, and institutions—came to be. As statesman and historian Winston Churchill put it, "Every nation or group of nations has its own tale to tell. Knowledge of the trials and struggles is necessary to all who would comprehend the problems, perils, challenges, and opportunities which confront us today." Thus, a study of history puts modern ideas and institutions in perspective. For example, though the founders of the United States were talented and creative thinkers, they clearly did not invent the concept of democracy. Instead, they adapted some democratic ideas that had originated in Ancient Greece and with which the Romans, the British, and others had experimented. An exploration of these cultures, then, reveals their very real connection to us through institutions that continue to shape our daily lives.

Another reason often given for studying history is the idea that lessons exist in the past from which contemporary societies can benefit and learn. This idea, although controversial, has always been an intriguing one for historians. Those that agree that society can benefit from the past often quote philosopher George Santayana's famous statement, "Those who cannot remember the past are condemned to repeat it." Historians who ascribe to Santayana's philosophy believe that, for example, studying the events that led up to the major world wars or other significant historical events would allow society to chart a different and more favorable course in the future.

Just as difficult as convincing students to realize the importance of studying history is the search for useful and interesting supplementary materials that present historical events in a context that can be easily understood. The volumes in Lucent Books' World History Series attempt to present a broad, balanced, and penetrating view of the march of history. Ancient Egypt's important wars and rulers, for example, are presented against the rich and colorful backdrop of Egyptian religious, social, and cultural developments. The series engages the reader by enhancing historical events with these cultural contexts. For example, in *Ancient Greece,* the text covers the role of women in that society. Slavery is discussed in *The Roman Republic,* as well as how slaves earned their freedom. The numerous and varied aspects of everyday life in these and other societies are explored in each volume of the series. Additionally, the series covers the major political, cultural, and philosophical ideas as the torch of civilization is passed from ancient Mesopotamia and Egypt, through Greece, Rome, Medieval Europe, and other world cultures, to the modern day.

The material in the series is formatted in a thorough, precise, and organized manner. Each volume offers the reader a comprehensive and clearly written overview of an important historical event or period. The topic under discussion is placed in a broad historical context. For example, *The Italian Renaissance* begins with a discussion of the High Middle Ages and the loss of central control that allowed certain Italian cities to develop artistically. The book ends by looking forward to the Reformation and interpreting the societal changes that grew out of the Renaissance. Thus, students are not only involved in an historical era, but also enveloped by the events leading up to that era and the events following it.

One important and unique feature in the World History Series is the primary and secondary source quotations that richly supplement each volume. These quotes are useful in a number of ways. First, they allow students access to sources they would not normally be exposed to because of the difficulty and obscurity of the original source. The quotations range from interesting anecdotes to far-sighted cultural perspectives and are drawn from historical witnesses both past and present. Second, the quotes demonstrate how and where historians themselves derive their information on the past as they strive to reach a consensus on historical events. Lastly, all of the quotes are footnoted, familiarizing students with the citation process and allowing them to verify quotes and/or look up the original source if the quote piques their interest.

Finally, the books in the World History Series provide a detailed launching point for further research. Each book contains a bibliography specifically geared toward student research. A second, annotated bibliography introduces students to all of the sources the author consulted when compiling the book. A chronology of important dates gives students an overview, at a glance, of the topic covered. Where applicable, a glossary of terms is included.

In short, the series is designed not only to acquaint readers with the basics of history, but also to make them aware that their lives are a part of an ongoing human saga. Perhaps they will then come to the same realization as famed historian Arnold Toynbee. In his monumental work, *A Study of History,* he suddenly became aware of history flowing through him "in a mighty current, and of his own life welling like a wave in the flow of this vast tide."

Important Events in the History of the Roman Republic

2000 B.C. 1000 B.C. 900 B.C. 800 B.C. 700 B.C. 600 B.C. 500 B.C. 400 B.C. 300 B.C. 200 B.C.

c. 2000
Primitive European tribes cross Alps into Italy.

c. 1200
Aeneas's legendary escape from burning Troy to Italy.

c. 1000
Latin tribes cross Alps and settle near Tiber River.

c. 850–700
Etruscans and Greeks settle in Italy.

753
Traditional but purely legendary date for Rome's founding.

c. 509
Romans expel their king and establish the republic.

494
Plebeians allowed to form their own Popular Assembly.

450
Roman laws written down in the Twelve Tables.

396
Romans sack the Etruscan town of Veii.

390
Barbarian Gauls attack and burn Rome.

367
Romans pass a law stating that one consul elected each year must be a plebeian.

326
Beginning of the Samnite Wars.

280–265
Romans defeat Greek cities and gain mastery of Italy.

264
First Punic War between Rome and Carthage begins.

241
Rome defeats Carthage, ending First Punic War.

229
Carthage's Hamilcar Barca dies.

221
Hannibal becomes leader of Carthage.

218
Hannibal crosses Alps into Italy; Second Punic War begins.

216
Hannibal defeats Romans in battle of Cannae.

204
Romans invade northern Africa.

202
Romans defeat Hannibal.

201
Romans defeat Carthage, ending Second Punic War.

197
Romans defeat Macedonia.

195
Roman women demand and get repeal of a law forbidding them to wear gold and fine clothing or to drive chariots.

190
Romans defeat armies of Seleucid ruler Antiochus III.

168
Romans defeat Macedonia in the Third Macedonian War.

146
Rome imposes direct rule on Macedonia and Greece; Romans destroy Carthage.

133
Tiberius Gracchus proposes land reforms and is killed by a mob.

123
Gaius Gracchus proposes land and citizenship reforms and is killed by a mob.

107
Gaius Marius is elected consul and begins reorganizing the army.

88
Rome grants citizenship to all free adult males in Italy.

82
Sulla becomes dictator.

77
Senate chooses Pompey to put down Sertorius's rebellious army in Spain.

73
Uprising of Roman slaves under Spartacus.

71
Crassus and Pompey defeat Spartacus.

67
Pompey clears the seas of pirates.

63
Cicero elected consul; exposes Catiline's plot to overthrow the republic.

60
Pompey, Crassus, and Caesar form First Triumvirate.

59
Caesar elected consul.

58–50
Caesar conquers Gaul.

49
Caesar crosses Rubicon River, beginning civil war.

48
Caesar defeats Pompey in battle of Pharsalus.

46
Caesar becomes dictator; Rome now a republic only in name.

44
Brutus, Cassius, and other senators assassinate Caesar.

43
Octavian, Antony, and Lepidus form Second Triumvirate.

42
Antony and Octavian defeat Brutus and Cassius in battle of Philippi, destroying last republican army.

33
Civil war between forces of Octavian and Antony.

31
Octavian defeats Antony and Cleopatra in battle of Actium.

27
Octavian takes title of Imperator Caesar Augustus; the Roman Empire begins.

A Genius for the Practical

Throughout history the greatest nations and peoples have displayed their own individual characteristics. They have evolved their own special ways of viewing the world around them and of dealing with that world. The ancient Greeks, for instance, were great originators and creators. They believed strongly in the worth of the individual and encouraged individual expression. They also loved beauty, which they saw everywhere in nature. The Greeks combined their individual creative energies with their love of beauty and produced magnificent original art, sculpture, architecture, and literature. The special genius that formed the basis of the Greeks' national character, then, was their creative spirit.

The Romans, on the other hand, produced few original cultural achievements. Wrote historian Edith Hamilton, "A sense of poetry was not strong in the Roman people. Their natural genius did not urge them on to artistic expression."[1] This was partly because the Romans viewed the individual less as a free spirit and more as a part of something greater and more important—society itself. In Rome the individual was subordinate to the system, the Roman state, which operated under fair but rigid and conservative laws. The Romans, striving above all else to be good law-abiding citizens, emphasized self-discipline over self-expression. They prized efficiency above creativity, and so they produced few original artists and writers.

Yet the Romans still managed to produce splendid cultural achievements, mainly because they were brilliant imitators. They regularly borrowed the most admirable aspects of the other civilizations they encountered. Speaking of his ancestors, the Roman historian Sallust admitted, "Whatever they found suitable among allies or foes, they put in practice at home with the

Some sections of Roman historian Sallust's (86–34 B.C.) History of the Roman Republic *still survive.*

The interior of the Colosseum in Rome, built in the first century A.D., in which the public watched men fight to the death.

greatest enthusiasm, preferring to imitate rather than envy the successful."[2] More than any other civilization, the Romans imitated the Greeks. Over the course of centuries Rome adopted Greek ideas about law, government, and religion, as well as Greek styles of sculpture, architecture, and literature.

But the Romans were not mere imitators. They had a profound ability to adapt the best ideas and inventions of others to their own needs with great efficiency. Often the Romans greatly improved upon the ideas and inventions they borrowed. And nearly always they judged an idea's worth by its usefulness. While the Greeks developed high culture to express their love of beauty, the Romans did so to meet the needs of society and the state. According to Edith Hamilton:

> Roman genius was called into action by the enormous practical needs of world empire. Rome met them magnificently. Buildings . . . where eighty thousand could watch a spectacle, baths where three thousand could bathe at the same time. . . . Bridges and aqueducts that spanned wide rivers. . . . That is the true art of Rome . . . its keen realization of and adaptation of practical means to practical ends.[3]

If, then, the Roman national character can be described in a single word, that word is practicality.

1 Village on the Tiber: Rome Is Established

The story of the Romans, a remarkable people who built the greatest empire in the ancient world, begins in ancient Italy. The geography and climate of this boot-shaped peninsula, which extends some five hundred miles southward from Europe into the Mediterranean Sea, were important

With his family's help, a Bronze-Age Italian warrior dons armor and weapons in preparation for battle.

factors in Rome's early development. In the north, the lofty, snow-covered Alps form a natural barrier separating Italy from the rest of Europe. While central Europe experiences harsh winters, Italy has a warm, pleasant climate most of the year. Several rivers, among them the Po, the Arno, and the Tiber, descend from the Apennines, the rugged mountains that stretch north-south through central Italy. On their way westward to the sea, these rivers pass through coastal plains and valleys covered in rich, productive soil. These warm, fertile regions of Italy attracted settlers from many parts of Europe and the Mediterranean. Among them were not only the ancestors of the Romans, but also other groups that would profoundly influence Roman culture and history.

The Perfect Place to Build a City

The first waves of settlers into Italy came from the north. As early as 2000 B.C. primitive tribes from central Europe began migrating southward across the Alps into the Po valley, where they established small farms and villages. Some of these cultures were Stone Age, using stone weapons and tools. Other slightly more advanced waves of immigrants had entered the European Bronze Age by the time they settled in Italy. They used implements made of bronze, a mixture of copper and tin.

In time, succeeding groups of European settlers pushed farther south into the plains of the Arno and Tiber rivers. Shortly before 1000 B.C. the Latin people settled in the region surrounding the Tiber River. They called this rich agricultural area nestled between the Apennines and the sea Latium. One tribe of Latins set up small communities on seven low hills clustered around a bend in the Tiber about fifteen miles inland from the sea. This location had a number of natural advantages. First, it was surrounded by fertile plains. In addition, it was at the center of trade routes moving west to east along the river and north to south along the western

The Roman historian Titus Livius (59 B.C.– A.D. 17), popularly known as Livy, wrote the 142-volume History of Rome.

border of the Apennines. In short, wrote the Roman historian Livy, the site on which Rome grew was a strategic location for a city:

> Not without good reason did gods and men choose this spot as the site of a city, with its bracing hills, its commodious [spacious] river, by means of which the produce of inland countries may be brought down and inland supplies obtained; a sea near enough for all useful purposes, but not so near as to be exposed to danger from foreign fleets; a district in the very center of Italy, in a word, a position singularly adapted by nature for the growth of a city.[4]

The first crude settlements in the area appeared on the three most prominent of the seven Roman hills—the Capitoline, the Palatine, and the Aventine. The exact dates and circumstances surrounding the origins of these settlements remain unclear. Later Romans accepted the date of 753 B.C. for the city's founding. But the Romans did not begin keeping regular historical records until the third century B.C. By that time the events of Rome's earliest years had become confused and shrouded in legend. Thus, the later Greek and Roman writers who tried to piece together Rome's early history often passed on differing and conflicting accounts. "From whom, and for what reason," wrote the Greek historian Plutarch, "the city of Rome, a name so great in glory, and famous in the mouths of all men, was so first called, authors do not agree."[5]

Eventually, one version of the city's founding became the most widely accepted. This legend claimed that the Romans were descended from Aeneas, a prince of the ancient city of Troy, located

Origins of the "Master Race"

By the second century B.C. many Roman writers and poets attempted to describe some aspect of Rome's founding involving the Trojan prince Aeneas or his descendants, Romulus and Remus. The most famous of these works was the long epic poem The Aeneid, *written by the poet Virgil between 30 and 20 B.C. In the opening Virgil describes Aeneas's escape from Troy. When the goddess Venus expresses her worry that Aeneas may not survive to land in Italy, Jupiter, king of the gods, assures her by revealing the future:*

"Since you are so consumed with anxiety for Aeneas,
I shall turn forward far
The hidden pages of fate and speak of the future.
He shall conduct a great campaign for you
And conquer all Italy and its haughty peoples.
He shall impose laws on his own people
And build walled cities for them; the third summer
Shall see him rule in Latium, the third winter
Of warfare see the Rutulians [an Italian tribe] subdued.
But his son Ascanius. . . .
It is he who shall consolidate your power—
For thirty years with all their turning months;
Then shall he move his capital from Lavinium
To Alba Longa, which he shall fortify
To the uttermost; and there a line of kings . . .
Shall reign and reign till Ilia, a priestess
Of royal blood, bear twins begotten by Mars;
And one of these, Romulus, fostered by a she-wolf,
And joyfully wearing her tawny hide, shall rule
And found a city for Mars, a new city,
And call his people Romans, after his name.
For them I see no measure nor date, I grant them
Dominion [power] without end. Yes, even Juno . . .
Even she will mend her ways and vie [agree] with me
In cherishing the Romans, the master-race,
The wearers of the Toga. So it is willed."

on the coast of Asia Minor, which is now Turkey. According to this story, when the Greeks sacked Troy about 1200 B.C., Aeneas escaped and sailed across the Mediterranean to the west coast of Italy. There he supposedly established a settlement near the Alban Mount, a steep hill about fifteen miles south of the Tiber.

Among Aeneas's descendants were twin boys named Romulus and Remus. A cruel king condemned the infant boys to be left outside to die. Soon, according to Livy,

a thirsty she-wolf from the surrounding hills, attracted by the crying of the children, came to them, and nursed them,

According to legend, Rome's founder Romulus and his brother Remus, after being abandoned as infants, survived when a wolf suckled them.

and was so gentle towards them that the king's flock-master found her licking the boys with her tongue. . . . He took the children to his hut and gave them to his wife to bring up.[6]

When Romulus and Remus reached adulthood, they decided to establish a city on the Tiber but fought over the exact location. Romulus built a wall on the Palatine hill and was angry when his brother climbed over it. Remus, wrote Livy, "was forthwith killed by the enraged Romulus, who exclaimed: 'So shall it be henceforth with everyone who leaps over my walls.' Romulus thus became sole ruler, and the city was called [Rome] after him, its founder."[7]

The story of Romulus's founding of Rome is largely fictitious. Modern archaeologists, scientists who unearth and study past civilizations, have found evidence that Latin settlements on the Roman hills were already thriving by 950 B.C. About 750 B.C. these separate communities merged into one city. It is possible that the dim memory of this important event later inspired the traditional 753 B.C. founding date.

The Importance of Family

The Latins who first settled the Roman hills had a relatively primitive culture. They lived in simple huts that had walls of dried mud and roofs made of thatch or bundled twigs and plant stalks. They could not read or write, produced no arts, and had no strong central government. From the beginning the family was the most important Roman social unit, and the male heads of families commanded the most power and respect in the community. Explains scholar Anthony Marks:

> Every family was led by a *paterfamilias* (father) and included his wife and children, and all their property and slaves. When the *paterfamilias* died, each of his sons might become the head of a new family, linked by name to the old one. The resulting chain of related families formed a clan called a *gens*.[8]

The names of the Roman clans usually ended in *ius,* for example, Fabius, Cornelius, and Julius. When Rome later became a great and prosperous city, many of the families bearing these time-honored names enjoyed much wealth and prestige.

Because the paterfamilias controlled all aspects of the lives of his family members, Roman society was completely dominated by adult males. Women and children, just as in most other ancient societies, had no rights and were not allowed to make important decisions for themselves. Nevertheless, a great amount of sincere, mutual love and respect existed in Roman families, especially between husbands and wives. Abundant evidence for this fact has survived in the form of thousands of later Roman tombstone inscriptions. "Stranger," wrote one grieving man,

> Here is the unbeautiful grave of a beautiful woman. Her parents named her Claudia. She loved her husband with her whole heart. . . . Her speech was gay, but her bearing seemly [proper and pleasing]. She kept the home. She made the wool. I have spoken. Go away.[9]

Other widowers left behind the messages:

> Here lies Amynone, wife of Marcus, most good and most beautiful, dutiful, modest, careful, chaste, stay-at-home.[10]

> To Aurelia Vercella, my wife most sweet, who lived seventeen years, more or less. . . . I have no more desires. Anthimus, her husband.[11]

The Contract with the Spirits

Just as a traditional, rigid family structure exerted a powerful influence over the lives of the early Romans, so did religion. Like other Latin tribes, the Romans worshipped spirits they thought resided in everything around them, including inanimate objects like rocks and trees. This kind of belief system is known as animism. At first the Romans pictured these spirits, called numina, as natural powers and forces rather than as thinking deities, or gods. In time, however, the spirits associated with some objects and natural phenomena began to take on humanlike personalities. These became gods and goddesses, such as Vesta, the spirit of the hearth fire, and Mars, who watched over farmers' fields.

In Rome's first few centuries there was no state religion involving public worship in temples. Religious ritual consisted of simple prayer and occasional animal sacrifices performed at home with the paterfamilias acting as priest. According to historian

The Romans eventually associated the god Mars with war and called him the Avenger.

Arthur Boak, the Romans believed that their relationship with their gods

> was of the nature of a contract. If man observed all the proper ritual in his worship, the god was bound to act propitiously [favorably]. . . . If man failed in his duty, the god punished him. . . . Thus Roman religion consisted essentially in the performance of ritual, wherein the correctness of the performance was the chief factor.[12]

Striving for correct forms of ritual, the Romans evolved a number of standard, traditional prayers and ceremonies. One of the most important was the prayer to Mars, consisting, in part, of the words:

> Father Mars, I pray and beseech thee, that thou mayest be gracious and favorable to me, to my home and my household, for which cause I have ordained [ordered] the offering [sacrifice] of pig, sheep, and ox . . . that thou mayest . . . ward off . . . all disease, visible and invisible, all . . . waste, misfortune, and ill weather; that thou mayest suffer our crops, our vines and bushes to grow and come to prosperity.[13]

Etruscan Influences

Roman religion, along with other aspects of Roman life, began to undergo significant changes between 850 and 700 B.C. During these years new waves of settlers discovered the pleasant climate and fertile soil of Italy and built cities near the region of Latium. Among them were the Etruscans,

The Mysterious and Artistic Etruscans

The Etruscans, who strongly influenced Rome's early history, were a fascinating people, partly because their origins remain mysterious. As historian Chester G. Starr explains in The Ancient Romans:

"Despite [an] abundance of archaeological evidence, the Etruscans are the subject of violent debates among modern scholars. . . . Some ancient writers considered the Etruscans to be of native Italian origins, as do some archaeologists today. The Greek historian Herodotus, on the other hand, told a story that they had left the Aegean [the sea bordering eastern Greece] in a time of famine; and most modern scholars feel that bands of Etruscans did make their way west, perhaps from Asia Minor, and settled in Etruria about 800 B.C. Although we can read the words in an Etruscan inscription, we cannot understand more than names, titles, and numbers; The Etruscan language was entirely different from Latin and other Italian tongues and has no certain relative anywhere."

The Etruscans produced many fine metal artifacts, including this bronze figure of a young girl.

lands located directly west of Italy, and with peoples all around the Mediterranean.

The Etruscans influenced the Romans in many ways. Through trade with Etruria, the Romans acquired many new goods, such as fine fabrics and pottery, that improved their standard of living. The Etruscans buried their dead in elaborate stone tombs. They also constructed numerous stone buildings, bridges, and sewer drains. The Romans learned Etruscan stonemasonry and other building techniques, including the use of the curved arch that eventually became a Roman trademark. The Romans also adopted some of the Etruscan gods. Among the most important were Jupiter, god of the sky, Juno, patron goddess of women, and Minerva, the goddess who protected craftspeople.

In addition, the Etruscans introduced political ideas to the Romans. Etruscan towns were ruled by individual kings, who

A bust of Juno, wife and sister of Jupiter, and goddess of women and childbirth.

who, because they were culturally more advanced than the Romans, strongly influenced Rome's early development. The original home of the Etruscans is still unknown, but some evidence suggests they came from Asia Minor. They settled in the region south of the Arno River and north of Latium, an area known then as Etruria and now as Tuscany. Both of these names are derived from the name of the people. The Etruscans were skilled craftspeople who practiced arts such as painting and sculpture and made pottery and jewelry. They made their living partly through agriculture, like the Romans, but also through trade. By land, Etruscan merchants traveled north into the Po valley and even beyond the Alps. By sea they traded with the inhabitants of Corsica and Sardinia, the large is-

An Industrious People

Whatever their origins, the Etruscans were an industrious and artistic people who were influenced by the Greeks. Some of the best preserved Etruscan art is in the form of tombs. According to historian Will Durant in Caesar and Christ:

"Those who could afford it were laid to rest in sarcophagi [coffins] of terra cotta [hardened clay] or stone, and the lid was topped with reclining figures carved partly in their likeness, partly in the smiling style of the [Greeks]. . . . Occasionally, the dead were cremated and placed in cinerary urns [urns for ashes], which also might be adorned with the figure of the deceased. In many cases the urn or tomb simulated a house; sometimes the tomb, cut into the rock, was divided into rooms, and was equipped for post-mortem [after death] living with furniture, utensils, vases, clothing, weapons, mirrors, cosmetics, and gems. In a tomb at Caere the skeleton of a warrior lay on a perfectly preserved bed of bronze, with weapons and chariots beside it; and in a chamber behind his were the ornaments and jewelry of a woman presumably his wife. The dust that had been her beloved body was clothed in her bridal robes."

Etruscan couples were often buried in coffins adorned with their likenesses. This sarcophagus is made of terra cotta, a hard ceramic clay.

held absolute power over their peoples. The Romans adopted this idea, and the first Roman king came to power about 750 B.C. when the original Roman villages united into a single city. If the first king was really named Romulus, as the legend claims, he was the strongest local paterfamilias of the day, rather than the city's founder. He was succeeded by Numa Pompilius, who, according to later legends, carried on traditional conservative Roman values such as seriousness, living simply, and religious devotion. Wrote Plutarch, "He banished all luxury and softness from his own home, and . . . in private he devoted himself not to amusement . . . but to the worship of the immortal gods."[14] Following Numa as Latin kings of Rome were Tullus Hostilius and Ancus Martius.

Sometime in the seventh century B.C. the Etruscans, either by threats or actual military force, took control of Rome. Three successive Etruscan kings—Tarquinius Priscus, Servius Tullius, and Tarquinius Superbus—ruled the city. But the takeover was not completely successful. While obeying their Etruscan masters, the Romans stubbornly continued to maintain their traditional customs, as well as the Latin language.

Greater Greece

Not long after the Etruscans settled in Italy, the Greeks followed. About 750 B.C. powerful Greek cities such as Athens, Corinth, and Miletus began establishing colonies around the Mediterranean. The Greeks built cities along the coasts of Sicily, the large island lying at the foot of the Italian boot, the most prosperous of

According to legend, Numa Pompilius, Rome's second king, was originally a member of the Sabine tribe.

these being Syracuse. They also settled in southern and western Italy. After a century of colonization, there were so many Greek towns in southern Italy that the Latins began calling the region Magna Graecia, or "Greater Greece."

The Greeks were even more culturally advanced than the Etruscans. The Romans, under both Latin and Etruscan rulers, were strongly influenced by Greek culture. Greek traders introduced systems of coinage and weights and measures. They also introduced their alphabet, much of which they had borrowed from the Phoenicians, a Middle Eastern trading people. This enabled the Romans to begin writing down their language. As historian James Henry Breasted describes it:

> Down at the dock below the Tiber bridge, ships from the Greek cities of the south were becoming more and more common. . . . The Roman trader

Athenian merchant ships like this one traded regularly with Greek cities in southern Italy.

had gradually learned to pick out the names of familiar objects of trade in the bills handed him by the Greek merchants. Ere long the Roman traders too were scribbling memoranda [business notes] of their own with the same Greek letters, which thus became likewise the Roman alphabet, slightly changed to suit the Latin language.[15]

The Greeks also influenced Roman religion. The Greeks had an elaborate collection of gods, many of whom the

Artemis, Greek goddess of the moon and hunting, rides her chariot through the sky.

Romans saw as counterparts of their own. For example, the Romans equated the powerful Greek god Zeus, who ruled the heavens, with their own sky god Jupiter. And Zeus's wife Hera, queen of the Greek gods, became the Roman goddess Juno. Inspired by the Greeks, the Romans enhanced the images of some existing gods. In this way, Mars, associated with the Greek war god Ares, became the Roman patron of warriors as well as protector of the fields. The Greek sea god Poseidon became the Roman god Neptune; Aphrodite, the Greek goddess of love, became Venus; and the Greek hunting goddess Artemis became Diana. The Romans also adopted completely new gods from the Greeks, such as Apollo, god of the sun, music, and healing.

Maintaining Old-Fashioned Values

In the days of the early kings, the Romans continued to view the Etruscans and Greeks as superior cultures to be imitated rather than as economic and military rivals. This

Organizing the Military

One of Rome's last kings, Servius Tullius, was remembered best by the later Romans for his organization of society into various classes. He formed these groups according to the amount of property people owned. Each class had certain social and political rights, but also certain duties and obligations, especially in wartime. In his History of Rome, *the Roman historian Livy recalls how Servius Tullius organized the structure of the military, a system that Rome used, with a few revisions, for some time to come:*

"He instituted the census, a most beneficial institution in what was to become a great empire. . . . From it he drew up the classes and centuries [groups of one hundred men] and the following distribution of them, adapted for either peace or war. Those whose property amounted to, or exceeded 100,000 lbs. weight of copper were formed into eighty centuries. . . . These were called the First Class. . . . The armor which they were to provide themselves with comprised helmet, round shield, greaves [metal leg protectors], and coat of mail [flexible armor], all of brass. . . . Their offensive weapons were spear and sword. To this class were joined two centuries of carpenters whose duty it was to work the engines of war; they were without arms. The Second Class consisted of those whose property amounted to between 75,000 and 100,000 lbs. weight of copper. . . . Their regulation arms were the same as those of the First Class, except that they had an oblong wooden shield instead of the round [brass] one and no coat of mail. The Third Class he formed of those whose property fell as low as 50,000 lbs. . . . The only difference in the armor was that they did not wear greaves. In the Fourth Class were those whose property did not fall below 25,000 lbs. . . . Their only arms were a spear and a javelin. The Fifth Class . . . carried slings and stones, and they included the supernumeraries [surplus troops], the horn-blowers, and the trumpeters, who formed three centuries. The Fifth Class was assessed at 11,000 lbs. The rest of the population whose property fell below this were formed into one century and were exempt from military service."

was because Rome was a small farming city that controlled only a portion of Latium. The Romans had no trading fleets of their own, so they could not compete effectively with the more powerful and prosperous peoples to the north and south. The lucrative trade routes and markets of the western Mediterranean were dominated by the Etruscans, the Greeks, and the Phoenicians. At about the same time that the Greeks

In galleys like this one, Phoenician traders sailed beyond the Strait of Gibraltar and founded towns on the western African coast.

colonized Italy and Sicily, the Phoenicians established their own colonies in Sicily and on other western Mediterranean coasts. One Phoenician colony, Carthage, located on the north African coast southwest of Sicily, quickly became the most prosperous trading center of the region.

While the Greeks, Etruscans, and Phoenicians controlled the trade routes, the Romans remained content to work their farms and maintain their traditional lifestyles. For centuries they had lived simple, practical lives built around family and community, with few frills and luxuries.

Although they acquired many new products and ideas from the Etruscans, Greeks, and others, the Romans preferred to maintain their old ways as much as possible. They adopted only those outside ideas and inventions that made their lives more efficient and their homes and families more secure. During these centuries the Romans strengthened the conservative values they most admired in themselves and in others. These included duty to family and community, respect for the gods, contempt for luxury and immorality, and a serious, dignified attitude toward self and life.

But while Roman values remained the same, by the end of the sixth century B.C. Roman political ideas began to undergo a dramatic change. Under Etruscan rule, the city had grown increasingly prosperous and some patresfamilias had become as rich as the kings. This new class of wealthy landowners, called patricians, demanded a greater say in government. During this same period a number of Greek cities threw out their kings and instituted governments run by groups of people. Such revolutionary political concepts inspired the Romans, especially the patricians. About the year 509 B.C. the Romans drove out their Etruscan king and established a republic, a government administered by popularly elected officials. Rome's spectacular rise from a backward village on the Tiber to master of the known world had begun.

2 Roman Republic: The Unification of Italy

When the Romans set up their republic in the late sixth century B.C., Rome was a small city-state that controlled only a tiny section of Italy. The city and its surrounding villages and farms covered a mere six hundred square miles, about the size of New York City. The total population of Roman territory at the time, including slaves, was perhaps 260,000. The Romans were hemmed in on all sides by other peoples. North of the Tiber stretched Etruria, still controlled by the powerful Etruscans, and directly south and east of Rome other Latin tribes held sway over the remainder of Latium. Farther east in the Apennine foothills lived primitive and fierce mountain tribes, including the Sabines, Umbrians, Volsci, and Aequi. Another Italian tribe, the warlike Samnites, controlled the area directly south of Latium, and the Greeks dominated Italy's southern coastal regions.

Surrounded by so many foes, the odds of Rome's very survival, much less its successful expansion, seemed small. Yet, in a little more than two centuries, Rome defeated all of these foes and took possession of all of Italy. The Romans accomplished this formidable feat mainly because they were highly organized and efficient, both militarily and politically. The Roman Republic

An early Roman town is surrounded by a defensive wall. This colony was one of many that Rome established in the fourth century B.C.

evolved by degrees into a strong, flexible government that answered the needs of most of its people. This instilled profound feelings of pride and patriotism in the Roman people. The Romans came to believe not only that their system was superior to those of their neighbors, but also that Rome's expansion and conquests were inspired by the gods. The combination of Roman efficiency and the belief that the Romans were divinely destined to conquer and rule others made Rome an unstoppable force in the early years of the republic.

Giving the People a Voice

Two major factors led to the overthrow of Rome's Etruscan kings and the establishment of the republic. First, the Romans had always resented Etruscan rule. Even though the Etruscans had transformed Rome from a backward village of simple farmers and mud huts into a thriving, trading city with merchants, craftspeople, and many fine stone buildings, the Romans never stopped seeing the Etruscan kings as foreign oppressors. The Romans longed for the day when they could expel the Etruscans and rule themselves.

The second factor was economic. Since the seventh century B.C., a group of the most respected patresfamilias, or patricians, had met periodically to discuss the problems of the community. Because they were also known as elders, or *senatores,* this group was called the Senate. At first, the senators had no real power and acted mainly as advisors to the kings. As some Roman farms grew large and successful in the sixth century B.C., however, the patricians who owned them became increasingly

A meeting of the early Roman Senate. Its membership grew from one hundred in the fifth century B.C. to six hundred in the first century B.C.

Lucius Junius Brutus, one of Rome's first two elected consuls, publicly denounces the former king and vows to support the new republic.

wealthy and powerful. Many became outspoken senators who succeeded in influencing some of the kings' decisions. Eventually, the patricians became powerful and bold enough to take complete control of the state. In 509 B.C., while King Tarquinius Superbus was away from the city, the Senate met, declared his rule null and void, and set up a new government. According to Livy, a popular patrician named Brutus spoke for the other senators when he declared publicly:

> I swear, and you, O gods, I call to witness, that I will drive [away] . . . Tarquinius Superbus, together with his wicked wife and his whole family, with fire and sword and every means in my power, and I will not suffer [allow] them or anyone else to reign in Rome.[16]

In setting up their republic, the Romans had two goals. The first was to create a system in which the people had a voice. The second goal was to divide the state's power among several people and groups in order to keep any single person from acquiring too much of that power. The Romans observed that some Greek cities had democratic assemblies, groups of citizens that met to discuss and vote on important issues and to elect leaders. The Romans adopted this idea, creating the Centuriate Assembly of citizens. Only free adult Roman men who owned weapons—those eligible for military service—were allowed to become citizens and participate in the Assembly. As in the Greek democracies, women, foreigners, and slaves had no say in government. Although many of the citizens who sat in the assembly were patricians, some were common people who did not own land but could still afford to own weapons. These plebeians, or plebs, made up the majority of males in the general population.

The Roman Assembly elected two governing officials called consuls. Explains historian Chester G. Starr:

> [These men] supervised the government at home and acted as generals abroad. Although in the field each consul usually operated independently with his own army, in Rome both had to concur [agree] if any serious political action was to be taken. In critical emergencies the consuls stepped aside to make way for a single dictator with overriding powers, who was appointed for 6 months.[17]

A dictator's term was short so that he could not abuse his power and try to rule permanently. Similarly, the consuls served

The Plebs Change an Unjust Law

In the early years of the Roman Republic, the plebeians, or plebs, demanded and won many political and legal reforms from the ruling patrician, or aristocratic, class. The plebeians often pressured the government into repealing unjust laws by refusing to serve in the military, a tactic that crippled the army and left the city open to attack. One particularly unfair law had allowed patrician creditors to enslave plebeians who could not pay their debts. In the following account taken from his History of Rome, *Livy tells how in the early fifth century B.C. the plebeians forced the Senate and a consul named Servilius to repeal this law.*

"The patricians and the plebeians were bitterly hostile to one another, owing mainly to the desperate condition of the debtors. They [the plebeians] loudly complained that whilst fighting in the field for liberty and empire they were oppressed and enslaved by their fellow-citizens at home. . . . The discontent . . . was further inflamed by the . . . misfortunes of one individual. An old man . . . suddenly appeared in the Forum. . . . His unkempt beard and hair made him look like a savage. In spite of this disfigurement he was recognized by the pitying bystanders; they said that he had been a centurion [military commander], and mentioned other military distinctions he possessed. . . . He was asked, 'Whence came that garb, whence that disfigurement?' He stated that whilst serving in the Sabine war he had . . . lost the produce of his land . . . his farm had been burnt . . . his cattle driven away . . . and he had got into debt. . . . He had been carried off by his creditor, not into slavery only, but into an underground workshop, a living death. Then he showed his back scored with recent marks of the lash. On seeing and hearing all this a great outcry arose. . . . It spread everywhere throughout the City. Men who were in bondage for debt and those who had been released rushed from all sides into the public streets. . . . Then they closed round the Senate-house. . . . In the middle of these disturbances, fresh alarm was created by some Latin horsemen . . . [who warned] that a Volscian army was on the march to attack the City. . . . The plebeians . . . said that the gods were preparing to avenge the tyranny of the patricians. . . . The consul Servilius . . . went into the Assembly of the plebs. . . . He convinced the Assembly of his sincerity by issuing an edict [official order] that none should keep a Roman citizen in chains . . . [preventing him] from enrolling for military service, none should . . . sell the goods of a soldier as long as he was in camp, or detain his children or grandchildren."

(Left) Roman government officials wore togas hemmed with ribbons of purple, the traditional color of royalty. (Top) A woman pleads her case before a praetor, *or court judge.*

for only one year so that if they were unpopular or did a poor job, they could be replaced quickly. The Senate remained as an advisory body to aid the consuls in making decisions. The senators, all well-to-do patricians, served for life.

In time the affairs of state became so complex that the consuls could not manage by themselves. So each year the Assembly elected various minor officials to help run the government. These included eight *praetores,* or court judges; four *aediles* to manage the streets and public buildings; two *censores,* responsible for census taking, enrolling new senators, inspecting morals and conduct, and collecting taxes; and twenty financial administrators called *quaestores.*

Gaining Veto Power

The new Roman government was not a true democracy like the ones in Athens and some other Greek cities, because only a privileged few took part in government. Since Roman public officials were not paid, only the well-to-do could afford to serve on a regular basis. Also, some political offices were closed to plebeians. In addition to patrician domination of the Senate, only patricians could become consuls. And the patricians controlled the Assembly through a system known as patronage, in which poor plebeians received financial or legal aid from wealthy patricians. In payment for this help, the plebeian *clientes,* "clients," voted in the Assembly as instructed by their patrician *patroni,* "patrons."

Many plebeians resented being excluded from the political process. Almost immediately after the creation of the republic, they began demanding more say in government. At first the patricians ignored their demands, but soon the plebeians went on strike, refusing to serve in the military. Without plebeian soldiers, the consuls could not raise the armies they needed to defend the city. Wrote Livy:

> The patricians dreaded the plebeians [who were striking]. . . . How long could it be supposed that the multitude which had seceded [struck] would remain inactive? And what would be the consequence if in the meantime a foreign war should break out? No glimpse of hope could they see left except in concord [agreement] between the citizens, which must be re-established in the state on any terms.[18]

Seeing no other choice, the patricians gave in. In 494 B.C., they allowed the plebeians to set up their own council, the Popular Assembly, which excluded patricians. Although this assembly lacked the power to make laws, each year it elected ten plebeian officials called tribunes to look after plebeian interests. The tribunes had the power to say *"Veto!"*, or "I forbid!" and stop the passage of any laws proposed by the patricians. "An accommodation [deal] was effected," Livy recalled, "on the terms that the plebeians should have magistrates [officials] of their own . . . who might have the power to afford them protection against the consuls; and that it should not be lawful for any of the patricians to hold that office."[19]

Rome's Twelve Tables listed laws covering money, property rights, family and inheritance, and public behavior.

A System Based on Law

In the following years the plebeians won other political concessions from the patricians. One of these concerned the law. Corrupt patrician judges often misquoted or altered the laws, which were still unwritten, in order to convict accused plebeians. In about 450 B.C., the plebeians ended this corruption by demanding that Rome's laws be written down. The result was the Twelve Tables, a list of rules that became the basis of Rome's fair and efficient legal system. Some of these laws dealt with trial procedures; for example:

> If plaintiff summons defendant to court, he shall go. If he does not go,

plaintiff shall call witness [to this]. Then only shall he take defendant [to court] by force.

Other laws related to rights of land ownership, such as:

Should a tree on a neighbor's farm be bent crooked by the wind and lean over your farm, you may . . . take legal action for removal of that tree.

Still other laws allowed people to sue for personal injury:

If he [the attacker] has broken or bruised [a] freeman's bone with hand or club, he shall undergo penalty of 300 pieces [of silver or gold].[20]

The plebeians later demanded and won other important rights. In 366 B.C., the consulship was opened to plebeians and it soon became a custom to elect one patrician and one plebeian consul each year. Finally, in 287 B.C., the Popular Assembly gained the power to make laws. While Rome was now a democracy in a technical sense, it never became a democracy in practice. Most plebeians still could not afford to quit their jobs to serve the state. And those who did often helped make ends meet by voting as instructed by wealthy patrician senators. Because the senators profoundly influenced the domestic and foreign policies of the consuls, Rome's real power still lay in the elite Senate.

Nevertheless, Roman citizens—even poor ones—still had a measurable voice in government. Most Romans viewed their system, one based on the rule of law, as fair and enlightened in comparison to the absolute monarchies in most other lands. Also, the Romans had created this system largely by peaceful compromise rather than by violent revolution. Proud of these accomplishments, most Romans were patriotic and willing to risk their lives to defend the state. Thus, the fairness and political flexibility of the republic made possible the strong and fiercely loyal Roman armies that set out to conquer all of Italy.

Early Roman Expansion

Early in the fifth century B.C., the Roman armies marched outward from northern Latium. Their first important military campaign was against the other Latin tribes, whom the Romans narrowly defeated in 496 B.C. near Lake Regillus, east of Rome. Little is known about this battle except that it gave the Romans control of most of Latium. Shortly afterward the Romans signed a treaty with the Latins, which stated in part:

Let there be peace between the Romans and all the Latin cities so long as heaven and earth are in the same place. Let them never make war on each other, nor call in foreign enemies . . . but let them help each other with all their force when attacked, and let each have an equal share of all the spoil and booty won in wars in common.[21]

Such lenient treatment of defeated peoples became a Roman tradition. Instead of imposing harsh, dictatorial rule on conquered enemies, the Romans drew up alliances with them and granted them either full Roman citizenship or a list of guaranteed rights. The Romans built roads and public buildings in the conquered lands. They also introduced the Latin language and Roman customs and otherwise

Roman Roads

As Roman territory in Italy greatly increased in size during the fourth century B.C., the Romans began building a network of well constructed roads. This network expanded as Rome's empire grew. According to scholars Anthony Marks and Graham Tingay in their book The Romans:

"The Romans developed their system of roads out of military necessity. In the early years of Rome's expansion, the army could march from the city to defend the frontiers in a few hours. As the empire grew, however, it became vital to move troops and supplies quickly over very long distances. The first major road, the *Via Appia,* [Appian Way] was begun in 312 B.C. It stretched south from Rome to Capua and took over 100 years to build. 900 years after its completion, the historian Procopius called it one of the great sights of the world. He noted that despite its age, none of the stones had broken or worn thin. The *Via Appia* was the first link in a network that eventually stretched over 85,000 km (50,000 miles) and reached every corner of the empire. Much later, the remains of these routes formed the basis of Europe's modern roads and railway lines. As well as helping the movement of troops, roads brought [the Romans] other changes. Merchants followed armies to sell to the troops, and later to the inhabitants of the new provinces. Trade flourished, and people and goods could quickly reach distant parts of the empire. So roads helped to unite the provinces, as well as to keep them under control."

The Via Appia *helped the Romans defeat the Samnites in the late fourth century B.C. by allowing swift transport of troops and supplies.*

Romanized defeated peoples, thus binding them to Rome. This wise and efficient method of administration made it easier to control conquered territories. It also instilled pride and patriotism toward Rome in the cities and territories the Romans absorbed. The Roman politician and writer Cicero explained why this made Rome strong and successful:

> Every citizen of a corporate town [one annexed by Rome] has, I take it, two fatherlands, that of which he is a native, and that of which he is a citizen. I will never deny my allegiance to my native town, only I will never forget that Rome is my greater Fatherland, and that my native town is but a portion of Rome.[22]

The Brink of Destruction

In the decades following Rome's defeat of the Latins, the republic was almost constantly involved in aggressive wars with its other neighbors. While fighting periodic battles with the Etruscans in the north, Roman armies moved into the Apennine foothills and clashed with the Sabines, Aequi, and Volsci. The Sabines fell to Rome by about 449 B.C., and the other tribes by the end of the century. The Romans then concentrated all of their energies on the struggle with their former masters, the Etruscans. In 396 B.C., after a ten-year siege, Rome sacked the important Etruscan stronghold of Veii, located about fifteen miles north of Rome.

The Romans now prepared for an all-out assault on the rest of Etruria. Before they could launch this assault, however, Rome met with a sudden catastrophe that brought it to the brink of total destruction. At the beginning of the fourth century B.C., the Gauls, a semicivilized, warlike people from central Europe, swept over the Alps into Italy. After pillaging and looting the towns of the Po valley, the invaders marched south and laid waste to much of Etruria.

This ornate coffin, known as the Amendola sarcophagus, depicts a battle between the Romans and the Gauls.

After defeating the Roman army at Allia, Gallic warriors loot a Roman temple and terrorize its priestesses.

Gauls were "struck with amazement" at the sight of so many white-bearded old men sitting quietly,

> without fear or concern.... The Gauls, for a great while, stood wondering at the strangeness of the sight, not daring to approach or touch them, taking them for an assembly of superior beings. But then one, bolder than the rest, drew near to one elderly Senator, and ... gently stroked his chin and touched his long beard; the Senator with his staff struck him a severe blow on the head; upon which the barbarian drew his sword and slew him. This was the introduction to the slaughter.[23]

The Gauls killed the other Senators and burned most of the city. In the following months, despite their grim losses, the

As the Gauls neared Rome, the Roman consuls assembled a large army to stop them. The two forces met on July 18, 390 B.C., near the Allia River, a few miles north of Rome. When the naked, long-haired, and fearsome-looking Gallic warriors staged a wild, screaming charge, the Romans, who had never witnessed such a spectacle, became terrified. They panicked and broke ranks, and in the confusion most of the Roman army was annihilated. From that time on, July 18 became known to the Romans as "the day of Allia," an unlucky date on the calendar.

The triumphant Gauls now entered the defenseless city of Rome and found that most of its inhabitants had fled into the countryside. A group of aging senators and former consuls boldly remained to face the attackers. According to Livy, the

The Gallic chieftain Brennus accepts the ransom from Roman leader Marcus Furius Camillus.

Roman people bravely rose to the challenge, appointing a general named Camillus as dictator. He quickly organized another Roman army and defeated the Gauls in a number of small skirmishes. The Gauls now agreed to withdraw to the north, providing the Romans paid them a large ransom in gold. The payment was made, and the invaders returned to the Po valley.

Master of Italy

Though severely shaken and weakened by the Gallic onslaught, the hardy and resourceful Romans steadily recovered and resumed their campaigns of expansion. They rebuilt the city, surrounded it with a defensive wall, and created new, better-trained armies. Between 380 and 338 B.C., Rome conquered many Apennine tribes to the east and south. The Romans vigorously Romanized these peoples, absorbing them into the Roman state, and year after year Roman territory, military strength, and determination grew.

Many Italian peoples became alarmed at Rome's aggressive policies. In 326 B.C., the fierce Samnites, worried about Roman expansion into south-central Italy, challenged the growing might of Rome. In time, the Gauls, Umbrians, and Etruscans

Humiliated by the Samnites

Rome's wars with the fierce Samnite hill warriors, which began in 326 B.C., were long and hard. In one of the war's first engagements, the Samnites captured an entire Roman army and forced the soldiers to give up their weapons and march back to Rome tied together like animals. The Romans never forgot this humiliating event. In his History of Rome *Livy described how the Roman soldiers felt:*

"There they were, looking at each other, gazing sadly at the armor and weapons which were soon to be given up, their right hands which were to be defenseless, their bodies which were to be at the mercy of their enemies. They pictured to themselves the hostile yoke, the taunts and insulting looks of the victors, their marching disarmed between the armed ranks [of Samnites], and then afterwards the miserable progress of an army in disgrace through the cities of their allies, their return to their country and their parents, whither their ancestors had so often returned in triumphal procession [victory parades]. While they were uttering these indignant protests, the hour of their humiliation arrived which was to make everything more bitter for them by actual experience than they had anticipated or imagined. First of all they were ordered to lay down their arms and go outside the rampart [defensive wall] with only one garment each."

Pyrrhus, king of Epirus, narrowly defeated the Romans in the battle of Ausculum in 279 B.C.

all joined the Samnites in a coordinated effort to defeat the Romans. After nearly forty years of bloody fighting, Rome decisively defeated these peoples and, by 285 B.C., controlled all of central Italy.

Now the Romans turned their attention to the Greek cities of southern Italy. Fearing a Roman attack, in 280 B.C. the Greeks asked Pyrrhus, ruler of the state of Epirus in northwestern Greece, for aid. Leading an army of some twenty thousand troops, Pyrrhus enjoyed some success against the Romans. But he lost as many battles as he won, and after five years of indecisive fighting he abandoned the war and returned to Epirus. The Greek cities of southern Italy could not match the Romans militarily and one by one they surrendered. By 265 B.C. Rome was the undisputed master of all Italy south of the Po River.

In two-and-a-half centuries of nearly relentless wars, Rome had risen from an obscure farming town to one of the world's great military powers. The efficiency and stability of the Roman government and the Roman people's ability to endure hardships had contributed significantly to this success. So had Rome's prudent administration of conquered peoples. Although the Romans themselves recognized these strengths, they were convinced that destiny was the main reason for their success. The gods, they believed, had proclaimed Roman mastery over other peoples. Cicero later summed up this view when he wrote, "We have overcome all the nations of the world, because we have realized that the world is directed and governed by the gods."[24] The Romans would soon find their self-proclaimed superiority severely tested. Their attempt to expand their influence into the western Mediterranean, a region controlled by powerful Carthage, would plunge them into a struggle for survival greater than any they had previously faced.

Chapter

3 Punic Wars: Rome and Carthage Battle for Supremacy

During the years that Rome was unifying Italy, the Phoenician city of Carthage in North Africa had grown into the chief trading center and most powerful city of the western Mediterranean. Carthaginian colonies and trading partners ringed the coasts of northern Africa, the islands of Corsica and Sardinia, and parts of Sicily. Carthage's large cargo and war fleets also controlled what is now southern France, eastern Spain and the Strait of Gibraltar at the extreme western edge of the Mediterranean. In the fourth century B.C. the Romans and Carthaginians had made a treaty, agreeing to stay out of each other's sphere of influence. At that time the Romans were not a seafaring people and were preoccupied with their conquests in Italy. So they took little interest in the Carthaginians, and the two peoples rarely came into contact.

However, when the Romans became masters of Italy in the early part of the third century B.C., they were not content to halt their expansion. They sought to push outward from the Italian peninsula and control some of the territories dominated by Carthage. This caused rivalry, hostility, and eventually armed conflict between the two great powers of the western Mediterranean. Rome and Carthage fought a series of bloody and costly wars for military, political, and economic supremacy. They

were called the Punic Wars after the Latin word *Punicus,* meaning Phoenician. Long before these conflicts between two equally ambitious rivals began, most Romans, Carthaginians, and their neighbors viewed such wars as inevitable. For instance, as he

Found in the modern African city of Tunis, this statue depicts a third-century B.C. Carthaginian man.

Pyrrhus's wins over the Romans were slim and costly. Such victories have been called "Pyrrhic" ever since.

led his army back to Epirus in 275 B.C., the Greek ruler Pyrrhus predicted the coming Roman-Carthaginian showdown, remarking, "How brave a field of war do we leave, my friends, for the Romans and Carthaginians

to fight in."[25] For both Rome and Carthage the wars developed into a bitter, all-out struggle for survival that could end only in the total destruction of one city-state and mastery of much of the Mediterranean world by the other.

Each Strong in a Different Way

In the early third century B.C. Rome and Carthage had much in common. Each ruled over a large territory inhabited by about three million people. Each had a large group of men that made laws and two chief administrators who ran the state. The Carthaginian counterparts to the Roman consuls were called *suffetes*. While the Romans had assemblies made up of both common people and aristocrats, the Carthaginian council of three hundred was composed entirely of aristocrats. That made Carthage an oligarchy, a government run by a select few. But these rulers made largely sound decisions that benefited the state and maintained the thriving economy of its trading empire. Therefore, like Rome, Carthage had a stable government that met most of the needs of its people. Both nations also possessed approximately equal military strength, although each was strong in a different way.

The strength of Rome's military lay in its army. In the early days of the republic, Roman armies were fairly small, and individual troops did not serve for very long. This was because many of the soldiers were citizen-farmers who could not afford to leave their homes for extended periods. This situation changed about 340 B.C. when the Romans began paying their soldiers

This quiet north African port was a busy Carthaginian naval base in the third century B.C.

for military service. Now, larger numbers of men could afford to be away from their farms for months at a time and receive extensive training. By the early third century B.C. Rome was able to field land forces totaling as many as 300,000 well trained troops, by far the largest and most formidable army in the Mediterranean world. Roman armies were divided into units of 4,000 to 5,000 men called legions. Each legion was made up of smaller units of about 100 men called centuries, each commanded by an officer known as a centurion. According to historian Frank Cowell:

> There were several degrees of rank and importance in the centurion class. The leading centurion (*primipilus*) was an officer of sufficient standing to attend a council of war. No common soldier could rise higher in the ranks than the position of leading centurion; that is to say he could never command a legion. The higher command was reserved for men of senatorial rank.[26]

By contrast, because they were primarily seafarers, the Carthaginians had little need for maintaining large standing armies. When Carthage required land troops, it hired mercenaries, foreign soldiers who fought in return for money. The nation's main power resided in its navies, consisting of the best ships and manned by the most experienced sailors in the Mediterranean. They could strike quickly and with devastating force against both rival shipping and coastal towns across the western Mediterranean. As a result, Carthaginian vessels controlled the seas, allowing Carthage to maintain a tight monopoly on trade in the region.

Thus, while Rome's economy was based on agriculture, Carthage thrived on the vast riches acquired by its fleets and merchants. Carthage spent a great deal of this wealth expanding and beautifying the city. "The city of Carthage itself was large and splendid," wrote James Henry Breasted.

It was in area three times as large as Rome. Behind wide docks and extensive

A few crumbling ruins are all that remain of Carthage, one of the great cities of the ancient world.

piers of masonry, teeming with ships and merchandise, the city spread far inland, with spacious markets and busy manufacturing quarters humming with industry. Beyond the dwellings of the poorer craftsmen and artisans rose the stately houses of the wealthy merchants, with luxuriant tropical gardens. Around the whole rose imposing walls and massive fortifications, enclosing the entire city and making its capture almost an impossibility. Behind the great city, outside the walls, stretched a wide expanse of waving palm groves and tropical plantations, dotted with the magnificent country houses of the splendid commercial lords of Carthage, who were to lead the coming struggle with Rome.[27]

Determination and a Secret Weapon

Constantly searching for ways to increase its wealth, Carthage was quick to take advantage of any situation that would expand its influence and power. It found just such an opportunity in 264 B.C. Syracuse, the largest of the Greek cities on Sicily, asked Carthage for help in its siege of the Greek city of Messina, at the northeastern tip of the island. Hoping to gain control of the strategic Strait of Messina between Sicily and Italy, Carthage complied and occupied Messina. Rome was uneasy about having its powerful and dangerous neighbor in charge of Italian coastal waters. Believing that this move violated the agreement to stay out of each other's respective spheres, Rome declared war.

Because Carthage controlled the seas and Rome had no war fleets, Carthage appeared to have a clear advantage as the First Punic War began. Carthaginian warships patrolled the eastern coasts of Sicily, bringing men, supplies, and weapons to Carthage's strongholds in the area. This prevented the Romans from successfully conquering the island. But the ever practical Romans, seeing the need for a fleet of their own, quickly built more than 120

Lowered onto the deck of a Carthaginian ship, a "crow" allows Roman troops to board and capture the enemy vessel.

A Roman trireme, *or warship, carrying over one hundred soldiers and as many as three hundred oarsmen, had a maximum speed of twelve miles per hour.*

large warships. Less than five years after the war began, they launched these ships, which were outfitted with a new Roman secret weapon called the *corvus,* or "crow." This was a long wooden gangway with a spike attached to the end. The crow stood in an upright position on a Roman ship until the vessel was next to an enemy ship. When the Romans lowered the crow onto the enemy's deck, the spike pierced the deck and held the gangway in place. Roman soldiers then poured across the crow onto the other ship. The building of the fleet and invention of the crow, wrote the ancient Greek historian Polybius,

> [show] us better than anything else how spirited and daring the Romans are when they are determined to do a thing. . . . They had never given a thought to a navy; yet when they had once conceived the project they took it

in hand so boldly that before gaining any experience in such matters they at once engaged [in naval battle] the Carthaginians, who for generations had held undisputed command of the sea.[28]

Rome won several naval victories against Carthage between 260 and 256 B.C., and the Romans seemed on the verge of winning the war.

Horrendous Losses

However, Rome soon lost its advantage. In 256 B.C. it landed an army of thirty thousand men, led by the consul Marcus Atilius Regulus, in North Africa, with the goal of attacking Carthage itself. The Carthaginians raised a large mercenary army and hired a skilled Greek general named Xanthippus to lead it. Xanthippus followed the Roman army at a distance as it plundered a number of Carthaginian villages. The wily Xanthippus waited until the Romans had completed a long march through an arid region and were thirsty and exhausted before he attacked. After hours of furious fighting, the Carthaginians were victorious. Most of the Romans were killed and a majority of the survivors, including Regulus, was taken prisoner.

During the next few years the Romans suffered other terrible disasters. One fleet after another was destroyed in violent storms at sea, because the upright crows made the vessels top-heavy and caused them to capsize. In all, Rome lost some six hundred warships and one thousand

Carthaginian war leader Hamilcar Barca. Between 237 and 229 B.C., he conquered Spain, a move the Romans found threatening.

troop transports. They also lost more than 100,000 men to drowning—more than any other navy in history.

The Carthaginians were able to inflict further defeats on the Romans. In 247 B.C. a brilliant war leader, Hamilcar Barca, called "the man of lightning," took charge of Carthage's forces. For years he raided the coasts of Sicily and Italy, harassing and humiliating the Romans. Making matters worse, Rome spent such huge sums of money waging the long war that by 245 B.C. the city was nearly bankrupt.

But, despite their horrendous losses the Romans refused to admit defeat. They courageously threw all of their remaining money, supplies, and manpower into building one last, large fleet. Commanded by the consul Gaius Lutatius Catulus, this fleet decisively defeated the Carthaginians off the coast of Sicily in 241 B.C. Suprised and devastated by this loss, Carthage begged for peace. The Romans demanded harsh terms, forcing the Carthaginians to give up both Sicily and Sardinia and also to pay Rome heavy tribute, or large sums of money, for the following ten years.

The Between-War Years

The victory over Carthage helped revitalize the war-weary Romans, providing them with a new burst of confidence in their own abilities. During the twenty years following the war, they renewed the policy of vigorous military expansion that had given them control of most of Italy. In a series of campaigns Rome conquered Illyria, now Albania, the region separated from eastern Italy by the narrow Adriatic Sea. Roman

Carthaginian merchants barter for goods, including a female slave, with wealthy Romans.

armies also attacked and defeated the Gauls in the Po valley, giving Rome control of most of extreme northern Italy.

Rome's economy also revived during these postwar decades. With Carthage defeated, Roman trade expanded around the Mediterranean and stimulated local Italian industries, such as shipbuilding, metalworking, and pottery and jewelry making. Some poor and middle-class merchants became rich, forming a new and powerful wealthy class—the "equestrian order." A number of equestrians became government officials and began to vie with wealthy patrician landowners for a share of political power.

While Rome prospered, the Carthaginians were not idle. While trying to rebuild his own nation's economy, beginning in 237 B.C., Hamilcar strengthened Carthage's trading partners in Iberia, now Spain. This brought Carthage large quantities of silver, copper, iron, agricultural products, and fish. Hamilcar may have intended to use Iberia as a base of operations for eventually renewing war with Rome. The Romans

apparently believed this was the case Polybius recorded their position, writing of Hamilcar:

> The result of the [First Punic] war in Sicily had not broken the spirit of that commander. He regarded himself as unconquered. . . . [He] never relaxed in his determined purpose of revenge and . . . set at once about securing the Carthaginian power in Iberia.[29]

Whether he was plotting a new war, there is no doubt that Hamilcar hated Rome. He imparted his anti-Roman feelings to his son Hannibal, who later recalled:

> My father . . . when I was a very little boy, only some nine years old . . . when he was going to take command in Spain . . . asked me "Whether I should like to go with him to [the army] camp?" As I . . . begged him not to delay taking me, he replied, "I will do so, if you will give the promise which I ask." Thereupon he . . . required me . . . to swear "That I would never hold friendship with the Romans."[30]

When Hamilcar accidentally drowned in 229 B.C., he was succeeded by his son-in-law Hasdrubal, who carried on Carthage's economic and military buildup. In 221 B.C. Hasdrubal was assassinated and Hannibal, at age twenty-six, took control of the Carthaginian armies. Hannibal became one of the greatest military leaders and strategists in history. Possessing a magnetic personality, strong personal discipline, and unmatched bravery, he inspired fierce loyalty in his troops. Wrote Livy:

> There was no other leader in whom the soldiers placed more confidence or under whom they showed more

An Alpine Pep Talk

Facing the prospect of marching across the freezing, snow-covered passes of the Alps in 218 B.C., most of Hannibal's men were reluctant. So he called a large number of his troops together and, using his well known persuasive skills, encouraged them. He reminded them that they had managed to cross the Pyrenees Mountains in northern Spain without incident and that they had often defeated the Gauls, who themselves had once sacked Rome. In History of Rome, *Livy quotes Hannibal as he asks the men:*

"What do you imagine the Alps to be other than lofty mountains? Suppose them to be higher than the peaks of the Pyrenees, surely no region in the world can touch the sky or be impassable to man. Even the Alps are inhabited and cultivated, animals are bred and reared there, their gorges and ravines can be traversed [crossed] by armies. What can be inaccessible to the soldier who carries nothing with him but his weapons of war? What toils and perils you went through for eight months to effect the capture of Saguntum [in Spain]! And now that Rome, the capital of the world, is your goal, can you deem anything so difficult or so arduous that it should prevent you from reaching it? Many years ago the Gauls captured . . . [Rome]; either you must confess yourselves inferior in courage and enterprise to a people whom you have conquered again and again, or else you must look forward to finishing your march on the ground between the Tiber and the walls of Rome."

Hannibal (247–183 B.C.) was one of history's greatest military leaders.

Hannibal rides an elephant in a victory parade, perhaps after defeating the Romans at the Trebia River in 218 B.C.

daring. He was fearless in exposing himself to danger. . . . No amount of exertion could cause him either bodily or mental fatigue. . . . He was by far the foremost [leader] both of the cavalry and the infantry, the first to enter the fight and the last to leave the field.[31]

Carrying on Carthaginian expansion in Iberia, in 219 B.C. Hannibal fearlessly attacked Saguntum, Rome's only ally in the region. The Romans interpreted this as proof that Carthage had been planning for years to reopen hostilities between the two nations. In 218 B.C. Rome sent ambassadors to Carthage with a stern ultimatum—surrender Hannibal to Rome or face its wrath. When the Carthaginians refused, Rome declared war.

Hannibal's Bold Strategy

Hannibal swiftly enacted a daring strategy. Instead of fighting the Romans at sea or in Africa, as Carthage had done in the First Punic War, he decided to bring the conflict to Roman soil. His goal was to invade Italy and defeat Rome's armies. After this, he believed, most of the peoples conquered by Rome, such as the Samnites and Gauls, would rebel and join him. In the fall of 218 B.C. Hannibal marched an army of twenty thousand infantry, six thousand cavalry, and forty elephants over the snow-covered Alps and entered the Po valley. The Carthaginians had long used elephants in battle, primarily to frighten enemies unused to the beasts. However, nearly all of Hannibal's

The Most Feared Generals

Although for a long time Hannibal knew no equal as a general, he recognized the competence of two Roman commanders—Fabius and Marcellus. They were the only generals Hannibal really feared during his days in Italy. As Plutarch put it in Lives:

"Marcellus was a man of action and high spirit, ready and bold with his own hand, and, as Homer [the Greek who recited the story of the Trojan War] describes his warriors, fierce, and delighting in fights. Boldness, enterprise, and daring to match those of Hannibal constituted his tactics, and marked his engagements. But Fabius believed that by following close and not fighting him, Hannibal and his army would be tired out and consumed, so that Hannibal found by experience that encountering the one, he met with a rapid, impetuous river, which drove him back; and by the other, though silently and quietly passing by him, he was insensibly washed away and consumed; and at last, was brought to this, that he dreaded Marcellus when he was in motion, and Fabius when he sat still."

elephants died on the journey to Italy, and they played no part in the war.

Hannibal's plan seemed to work almost immediately. The recently conquered Gauls were only too happy to cast off Roman rule and help the Carthaginians. Seeking to defeat Hannibal quickly and decisively, the Roman consuls Scipio and Longus attacked him near the Trebia River, several miles south of the Po River, in December 218 B.C. But the wily Hannibal, expecting the assault, laid an ambush, and the Carthaginians destroyed more than two-thirds of the Roman army. A few months later Hannibal defeated another Roman army near Lake Trasimene, in north-central Italy. Nearly two entire Roman legions and their commander, the new consul Gaius Flaminius, were annihilated in the battle.

In desperation, the Romans appointed a senator named Fabius Maximus as dictator. Fabius wisely refrained from risking his troops in battle with Hannibal. Instead he followed Hannibal's army over the course of many months, harassing the enemy and making it hard for the Carthaginians to gather needed supplies. Such delaying tactics have been called "Fabian" ever since. Meanwhile, Hannibal waited for the Italians to form a widespread revolt against Rome that never seemed to come.

Catastrophe at Cannae

In 216 B.C., when Fabius's term as dictator expired, the Romans elected Paullus and

Varro as consuls. In the summer the two leaders led a well trained army of sixty thousand men to Cannae, in southeastern Italy, where Hannibal was camped with forty-five thousand Carthaginians and Gauls. On August 2 the armies faced each other on a flat plain near Cannae. Hannibal ordered most of his army to form a long, thin line but kept his cavalry stationed on the far right and left sides, or flanks. Then, as Chester Starr describes it:

> The battle began. Hannibal stood in the center of his line, where he had stationed his . . . Spanish and Gallic infantry, and personally supervised their slow, planned retreat before . . . heavy Roman pressure. While he thus lured the Romans forward, the Carthaginian cavalry won first on the left flank, then on the right flank. Thereupon . . . his cavalry closed behind the rear of the close-packed Roman infantry, which was blinded by the summer dust kicked up on the dry plain. Only about 10,000 Romans managed to break their way out of the trap. This double envelopment on both flanks of a numerically superior enemy was one of the greatest tactical masterpieces in all military history.[32]

When news of the disaster at Cannae reached Rome, fear gripped the city. At least fifty thousand men had died in the battle, including the consul Paullus and some eighty senators. There was a widespread outpouring of grief as the lists of the dead were read in the streets. Yet, as they had done so often in the past, the Roman people, poised at the brink of ruin, met the crisis with courage, discipline, and dignity. They maintained a fighting spirit and rallied around the defeated consul Varro when he returned. Recalled Livy:

> In spite of all their disasters [at Hannibal's hands] no one anywhere in Rome mentioned the word "Peace," either before the consul's return or after his arrival. . . . Such a lofty spirit did the citizens exhibit . . . that though the consul was coming back from a terrible defeat for which they knew he was mainly responsible, he was met by a vast concourse [crowd] drawn from every class of society, and thanks were formally voted to him because he "had not despaired of [deserted] the republic."[33]

Master of the Western Mediterranean

With victory seemingly within his grasp, Hannibal never achieved his ultimate goal of ending Roman power. It remains unclear why he did not follow up his great victory at Cannae with an attack on Rome itself. Perhaps he felt that a siege against so large and populous a city would fail. Apparently he was still sure that Rome's subjects would rebel, so he waited. Although a few southern Italian peoples revolted, as the Gauls had, most Roman subjects remained loyal.

For the next thirteen years Hannibal roamed Italy, while the Romans repeatedly used Fabian tactics and avoided fighting him. When Rome carried the war to Africa in 204 B.C., Hannibal finally returned to defend his native land. In 202 B.C., on the plain of Zama, southwest of Carthage, he was finally defeated by a brilliant Roman commander named Scipio Africanus, who used some of Hannibal's own tactics against him.

Roman Respect for Hannibal

Although the Romans usually characterized their Carthaginian enemies as cruel, barbaric, and without redeeming features, most Roman writers recognized and respected Hannibal's qualities as a leader and praised him. In his History of Rome, *Roman historian Livy describes Hannibal:*

"I hardly know whether Hannibal was more wonderful when fortune was against him than in his hours of success. Fighting for thirteen years in enemy territory, far from home, with varying fortunes and an army composed not of native troops but of a hotch-potch of the riff-raff of all nationalities, men who shared neither law nor custom nor language, who differed in manner, in dress, in equipment, who had in common neither the forms of religious observance nor even the gods they served, he yet was able, somehow or other, to weld this motley [mixed] crowd so firmly together that they never quarrelled amongst themselves nor mutinied against their general, though money to pay them was often lacking and provisions to feed them were often short."

In 196 B.C., Hannibal fled to Syria and later, to Bithynia in Asia Minor. As pictured below, he committed suicide there in 183 B.C.

The second defeat of Carthage was Rome's greatest achievement to date. In the peace treaty signed in 201 B.C., the defeated Carthaginians surrendered to Rome all but ten of their warships, the whole land of Iberia, and most of their other territories. Pursued by hostile Romans, Hannibal fled to the eastern Mediterranean where he eventually committed suicide.

Rome was now the undisputed master of the western Mediterranean and the greatest military power in the known world. But many Romans were not convinced that their troubles with Carthage were over. They felt that as long as Carthage existed, it would pose a threat to Rome. In time Rome would deal with this problem with unprecedented coldness and brutality.

4 Conquest and Expansion: The Mediterranean Becomes a Roman Lake

After defeating Carthage a second time, Rome became the dominant power in the western and central Mediterranean. Roman territory included Italy, the islands of Sicily, Sardinia, and Corsica, all of Iberia, and Illyria, directly north of Macedonia and Greece. After many years of successful wars of expansion, many Romans had become imperialistic—they favored the policy of using military threats and force to extend their power and influence. A group of Roman politicians, led by the popular general Scipio Africanus, advocated the conquest of Macedonia, Greece, and other eastern Mediterranean regions. A more conservative group, led by the senator Cato the Elder, was against expanding eastward. Cato argued that governing so many faraway lands would be too difficult and would waste Roman money and manpower. In the first half of the second century B.C., Rome enacted what was essentially a compromise between these two positions. The Romans conquered many of the eastern lands but at first did not impose direct rule on them. Instead, it made them into vassal states, territories that could rule themselves as long as they supported and did the bidding of Rome.

For Rome this period of rapidly shifting foreign affairs was also one of significant internal change. As the city's new empire grew, so did trade. Wealth from one end of the Mediterranean to the other flowed into Italy, stimulating the desire for luxuries most Romans were not accustomed to.

Publius Cornelius Scipio, known as Scipio Africanus, defeated Hannibal, then helped conquer the Greek Seleucid kingdom.

Cato's Advice to Farmers

Cato's On Agriculture *was written as a guide to running one of the many* latifundia, *or large estates, that dotted the fertile plains of Italy in the second century* B.C. *The work reveals much about Roman customs and practices of the time. In the following three excerpts, Cato explains how much to feed the estate's slaves, how to keep moths away from clothes, and the proper sacrifices to ensure the favor of the gods before a harvest:*

"Bread rations for the slaves. For those who do the field work, four *modii* [measures] of wheat in winter, four and one-half in summer; for the foreman, the foreman's wife, the overseer and the shepherd, three *modii;* for the slaves working in chains, four pounds of bread in winter, five when they begin to dig the vineyard, until there begin to be figs, then go back to four pounds.

■ ■ ■ ■

To keep moths from touching clothes: Boil old dregs [oil sediments] down to half and dress with them [rub them on] the bottom of the [storage] chest and the outside and the feet and the corners. When it has dried, put the clothes in it. If you do this, moths will do no injury. And if you dress any kind of wooden furniture in the same way it will not decay and when you polish it, it will be brighter.

■ ■ ■ ■

Before you make the harvest you should offer a preliminary sacrifice of a sow pig in the following way. Offer a sow pig to [the god] Ceres before you store away these crops: spelt [a reddish wheat], wheat, barley, beans, rape seed. First, address [the gods] Janus, Jupiter and Juno with incense and wine before you sacrifice the sow pig. Offer a sacrificial cake to Janus with these words: 'Father Janus, in offering to thee this sacrificial cake I make good prayers that thou will be kind and favorable to me, my children, and my house and household.'"

Cato the Elder (234–149 B.C.) was called the "censor" for promoting traditional conservative values.

The upper classes, into whose pockets most of this wealth flowed, enjoyed these luxuries and also used some of their money to support the arts, literature, and theater. Because only a few people had most of the money, the gap between rich and poor widened. Poor people seeking jobs or new lives flocked to Rome from all parts of Italy and the Mediterranean world, and the city became large and crowded. Many immigrants did not come willingly. During their conquest of Greece, for example, the Romans captured thousands of Greeks and forced them to work as slaves for well-to-do Roman families in Italy.

Wars in the East

Rome's troubles with the Greeks began during the Second Punic War. While his armies had ravaged Italy, Hannibal had requested help from King Philip V of Macedonia. At the time, Macedonia was one of three large Greek kingdoms ruled by the descendants of the Greek conqueror Alexander the Great. Alexander had defeated the Persians in the fourth century B.C. and created a vast empire stretching from Greece to India. But shortly after his death his generals fought among themselves and divided up that empire. The Macedonian kingdom included the city-states of Greece, the islands of the Aegean Sea, and parts of Asia Minor. The Seleucid kingdom encompassed Syria, Palestine, and other Middle Eastern lands that had once been part of the Persian Empire. The Ptolemaic kingdom consisted principally of Egypt. These kingdoms frequently fought one another in costly and indecisive wars. But they feared the growing power of Rome more than they feared each

The Greek general Alexander the Great created an empire that stretched from Greece to India in the fourth century B.C.

other. Hoping to see the Carthaginians eliminate the Roman threat, Philip responded to Hannibal's plea for help by sending ships and supplies from Macedonia.

Once they had defeated Carthage, the Romans, led by Scipio Africanus, sought revenge against Macedonia. In 200 B.C. Scipio led several legions against Philip's forces. In less than three years, the Romans crushed the Greeks and transformed Philip's kingdom into a helpless vassal state. According to Livy:

> Peace was then granted to Philip on the following terms: All the [Macedonian] communities in Europe and Asia were to be free and independent. . . . The King was also to restore all prisoners to the Romans, and all his decked ships, save five, were to be surrendered, but

he could retain his royal galley. . . . His army was never to exceed five thousand men and he was not allowed to have a single elephant, nor was he permitted to make war beyond his frontiers [borders] without the express sanction [permission] of the Senate. He was also required to pay a heavy indemnity [large sum of money].³⁴

Rome next turned on the Seleucid kingdom. The Romans, now boldly imperialistic, looked for any excuse, no matter how minor, to justify an attack. In 192 B.C., the Seleucid king, Antiochus III, took over some of the Greek cities that had been freed after the war between Rome and Macedonia. Rome immediately sent troops into Greece and forced Antiochus to flee with his own soldiers to Asia Minor. The

The Seleucid ruler Antiochus III was first defeated by the Romans at Thermopylae in Greece in 191 B.C.

Romans gave chase and in 190 B.C. they decisively defeated Antiochus near Magnesia in western Asia Minor. Sections of the Seleucid kingdom, largely in Asia Minor, now became vassal states to Rome in the same manner as Macedonia.

The Circle of Popilius

This last victory did not end Rome's troubles with the Greeks, however. In 171 B.C. another Macedonian leader, Perseus, plotted with a number of Greek city-states against Rome. The Romans responded by sending more armies to Greece, and they demolished Perseus's forces in 168 B.C. In the meantime, another Seleucid ruler, Antiochus V, hoping to revitalize his kingdom and challenge Roman power in the east, invaded Egypt. Wasting no time, early in 167 B.C. the Roman Senate ordered an ambassador named Gaius Popilius Laenas to Egypt with an ultimatum. When Antiochus greeted Popilius and went to shake hands, wrote Polybius:

> Popilius answered by holding out the tablets which contained the decree of the Senate, and bade Antiochus read that first. . . . Popilius [then] did a thing which was looked upon as exceedingly overbearing and insolent [insulting]. Happening to have a vine stick in his hand, he drew a circle around Antiochus with it, and ordered him to give his answer to the letter before he stepped out of that circumference. The king was taken aback [shocked] by this haughty proceeding. After a brief interval of embarrassed silence, he replied that he would do whatever the Romans demanded.³⁵

Popilius then demanded that Antiochus and his troops leave Egypt immediately. Fearing the same fate as Perseus and the other Greeks who had stood up to Rome, Antiochus complied. Thus, the Seleucids remained subject to Rome and Ptolemaic Egypt became a Roman vassal state, all without a fight.

The showdown in Egypt, thereafter referred to as "the circle of Popilius," became a symbol of Roman power and arrogance. For the next twenty years the Greeks did not dare challenge Rome's supremacy in the region. Then, in 146 B.C., two Greek cities, Sparta and Corinth, quarreled with each other and Rome sent envoys to settle the dispute. Unhappy with the settlement, the Corinthians made the mistake of attacking the envoys. Rome responded swiftly and harshly. As a lesson to other Greeks, Roman soldiers attacked Corinth, massacred most of the inhabitants, enslaved the survivors, and burned the city to the ground. Despite Cato's warnings that imposing direct rule was a mistake, Rome did so, abolishing all democracies in Greece and making Macedonia a Roman province.

Rich and Poor

While Rome conquered the Greeks and turned the entire Mediterranean into a Roman lake, all trade in that area came under Roman control. The money from increased trade, as well as from the gold, jewels, and other riches plundered from conquered peoples, made Rome more prosperous than ever. But with this prosperity came many problems. A small class of patricians, equestrians, and other landowners and merchants became richer than ever, while the majority of people remained poor. And the number of poor grew steadily larger. One reason for this was that rich patrician farmers used their new wealth to buy large tracts of land and create huge estates called *latifundia*. Unable to compete, most small landowners gave up and migrated to the cities, especially Rome, in search of jobs.

Roman general Lucius Mummius oversees the plunder and destruction of the Greek city of Corinth in 146 B.C.

As a result, Rome grew large, crowded, dirty, and noisy. The poor were packed into urban tenements, run-down apartment buildings with small rooms and little sanitation. To meet the demand of the increasing population of poor, the owners of these buildings often added extra floors. Because they were so poorly constructed, the tenements frequently collapsed, killing or maiming the inhabitants. The streets also became congested, sometimes unbearably so, a condition that would endure in Rome for centuries to come. Describing his daily ordeal in pedestrian traffic, the Roman writer Juvenal recalled in his *Satires*:

> I hurry but there's a wave ahead of me in the way, and the crowd is so dense the people behind jam against my back

Rush hour on the Via Appia *near Rome. The structures depicted are the tombs of wealthy Roman families.*

In his writings, Juvenal (c. A.D. 60–130) bitterly but humorously attacked Roman poverty and injustice.

and sides. Someone rams me with his elbow, someone else with a pole, this fellow cracks my head with a two-by-four, that one with a ten-gallon jug, my shins are thick with mud, now I'm being trampled by somebody's big feet—and there goes a soldier's hobnail in my toe![36]

At night, however, the streets of Rome were nearly deserted because they were dark and unsafe. A fight with a mugger or thief was a harrowing experience, said Juvenal,

> if it's fighting when he does all of the punching and all you do is get hit. He stands in your way and orders you to stop, and you've got to obey; what can you do when you're being forced by someone raging mad and, what's more, stronger than you are?. . . It makes no difference whether you try to say something or retreat without a word, they beat you up all the same. . . . You know what the poor man's freedom

amounts to? The freedom, after being punched and pounded to pieces, to beg and implore that he be allowed to go home with a few teeth left.[37]

The rich, on the other hand, could afford to employ packs of bodyguards or servants to protect them if they wanted to go out at night. This was only one way in which the lives of the wealthy were markedly different from those of the poor.

While tenement-filled slums sprang up in some sections of Rome, elegant upper-class houses were built in other areas. For centuries, Roman houses, even those of the well-to-do, had been relatively small, practical, and plainly decorated inside. But during the Macedonian wars, the Romans saw and admired the large, comfortable houses of the wealthier Greeks. Greatly influenced by Greek life-styles, upper-class Romans began enlarging and adorning their own dwellings. It became the fashion to fill a fine home with elaborate furniture, paintings, sculptures, and other luxuries plundered from Greek houses. Roman soldiers, explained Livy,

brought into Rome for the first time bronze couches, costly coverlets, bed curtains, and other fabrics, and—what was at that time considered gorgeous furniture—one legged tables and sideboards.[38]

Con Artists and Women's Rights

The new luxurious life-styles of the rich became extremely attractive to those without wealth. Seeking to marry into wealthy

Rome Plunders Its Enemies

The Romans frequently looted conquered peoples. In his Histories, *Polybius tells how a general named Paullus plundered the Greek state of Epirus while marching back from the Macedonian wars:*

"Early in the morning all the treasure was collected; at the fourth hour the signal was given to the soldiers to plunder, and so ample was the booty acquired that the shares distributed were four hundred denarii [silver coins] to a horseman and two hundred to a footman. One hundred and fifty thousand persons were led away captive. Then the walls of the plundered cities, in number about seventy, were razed, the effects [goods] sold, and the soldiers' shares paid out of the price. . . . The total of the captured gold and silver carried in the [triumphal] procession [at Rome] was one hundred and twenty millions of sesterces."

families, many middle-class young men became smooth-talking fortune hunters who preyed on the daughters of rich patres-familias. The poet Martial described one such young con artist:

> Gemellus is doing all he can to make Maronilla his bride.
> He showers gifts, he sighs, he groans, he begs her to decide.
> "I suppose she's very beautiful." "God, no! Her looks could kill."
> "Then what's produced this passionate love?" "A codicil [inheritance clause] in her will."[39]

Wealth also indirectly stimulated the growth of women's rights in Rome. Believing that luxuries would spoil women and make them disobey their husbands and fathers, lawmakers had passed a special law in the third century B.C. This law forbade women from wearing gold, beautiful clothes, or driving chariots. In 195 B.C. thousands of middle-class and wealthy women entered the Senate and boldly demanded the law be repealed. Cato, fearing this was the first step in a feminist drive for equality, led the opposition to this change. "From the moment that they become your equals," he warned, "they will be your masters."[40] The law was repealed, however. Confirming Cato's worry, other laws restricting women, both rich and poor, were struck down in the following decades. Although women did not gain political rights, they did win the rights to handle their own money and to sue their husbands for divorce. Roman women came to enjoy far more personal freedoms than Greek women did. In Greece, the land whose customs so many Romans now copied, each woman mostly stayed at home and did their husband's bidding.

Art and Literature

The Romans felt Greek influence in much more than their homes, furnishings, and personal luxuries. Roman architects began openly copying Greek architecture, and Greek-style temples, theaters, and government buildings sprang up by the hundreds all over Italy. Greek art and sculpture was so admired in Rome that many wealthy Romans became patrons of the arts. They generously supported hundreds of Roman artists who turned out copies of Greek originals for Roman homes, temples, and public buildings. The Romans, who had produced no significant literature before this period, also began turning out writings in Greek literary styles. The most notable writers of the day were the playwrights Terence and Plautus, who wrote mostly slapstick comedies based on well known Greek plays. Typical of the zany antics in these works is the following scene from Plautus's *The Merchant*. A young man who has brought home a young girl becomes distressed when his slave informs him that his father is making a play for her.

> SLAVE. Terrible—dreadful—awful— awful news—Oh, it's bad, bad.
> YOUNG MAN. Speak it out. What *is* the matter? Don't dare say bad news again.
> SLAVE. Oh, don't ask me. It's too awful.
> YOUNG MAN. By the Lord, you'll be so thrashed [beaten]—
> SLAVE. If I must, I must. Your father—
> YOUNG MAN. (terrified) Father! What?
> SLAVE. He saw the girl.
> YOUNG MAN. Hell! How could he?
> SLAVE. With his eyes.
> YOUNG MAN. But how, you fool?

Human Nature Then and Now

The plays of Plautus and Terence contain abundant humor, and pointed observations of human nature. The following speech from Terence's The Phormio *reveals that the Romans were no different from people today. When a young man named Antipho, who enjoys a happy marriage and carefree life, begins complaining, his cousin Phaedria lectures him, saying:*

"See here, Antipho, some people feel bad because they don't possess the object of their affections; you seem to be suffering because you've got too much of yours. You're simply embarrassed with bliss, Antipho. So help me Heaven, I swear, this life of yours is what all men covet and desire. Bless *me!* I'd sell my life right on the spot if I could have *my* sweetheart as long as you've had yours already. Just you try to imagine the other side of the picture, all that I'm suffering now from privation [being alone], and all that you're enjoying from possession [of your wife]; to say nothing of the fact that, without any expense, you've found a well-born and well-bred lady, that you can acknowledge her openly as your wife, without any scandal—a perfectly happy man but for one thing, a disposition to take it all and be content. Why, if you had anything to do with a slave-dealer like mine, then you'd find out! But that's the way most all of us are made; always feeling sorry for ourselves!"

The six known plays of Terence (c. 195–159 B.C.), adapted from Greek comedies, later influenced English and French playwrights.

SLAVE. By opening 'em.

YOUNG MAN. Damn you, quibbling [fooling around] when my life's at stake.

SLAVE. Oh, cheer up. Worse to come.

Soon's he saw her, the old blackguard [scoundrel] started petting [fondling].

YOUNG MAN. Heavens! Her?

SLAVE. Strange it wasn't me—[41]

Other important writers of the day were Polybius, the historian, a captured Greek who later won his freedom and acquired Roman citizenship, and Cato, the influential senator. Polybius attempted to record the events, past and present, that shaped the Mediterranean world he lived in. His unbiased and largely accurate work *Histories* remains an important eyewitness account of Roman life. Cato's most famous work, *On Agriculture*, a handbook on how to run a large estate efficiently, was Rome's first important long prose work.

Roman Discipline and Honesty

Polybius, a Greek who became a Roman, had the advantage of seeing the best and worst of both civilizations. He became convinced that, while the Greeks were more creative than the Romans, the Romans were far more disciplined and honest. These qualities, he believed, came partly from the Romans' strong religious beliefs. By contrast, he pointed out, many Greeks at the time no longer believed in the gods, and their abandonment of religion had made them untrustworthy. Wrote Polybius in his Histories:

"The quality in which the Roman commonwealth [nation] is most distinctly superior is in my opinion the nature of their religious convictions. I believe that it is the very thing which among other peoples is an object of reproach [scorn], I mean superstition, which maintains the cohesion [unity] of the Roman State. . . . My own opinion at least is that they have adopted this course for the sake of the common people. It is a course that perhaps would not have been necessary had it been possible to form a state composed of wise men, but as every multitude [large group of people] is fickle, full of lawless desires, unreasoned passion, and violent anger, the multitude must be held in by invisible terrors and suchlike pageantry [ceremonies]. For this reason I think, not that the ancients acted rashly . . . in introducing among the people notions concerning the gods and beliefs in the terrors of hell, but that the moderns are most rash and foolish in banishing such beliefs. The consequence is that among the Greeks . . . members of government . . . [often] cannot keep their faith [and end up stealing public money]; whereas among the Romans those who as magistrates . . . are dealing with large sums of money maintain correct conduct just because they have pledged their faith by oath. Whereas elsewhere it is a rare thing to find a man who keeps his hands off public money . . . among the Romans one rarely comes across a man who has been detected in such conduct."

Carthage Must Be Destroyed

Cato was even more famous for his oratory, particularly his speeches condemning Carthage. He and other conservatives believed that Rome had been too lenient on the Carthaginians at the end of the Second Punic War. Cato insisted that as long as Carthage existed it remained a dire threat to Rome. To emphasize his point he ended every public speech, no matter what the subject, with the words, "Carthage must be destroyed!"

Eventually, Cato's desire was fulfilled. Since its defeat in 201 B.C., Carthage had struggled to survive in the Mediterranean's Roman-dominated markets. Trying not to provoke the Romans, the Carthaginians had honored the treaty and refrained from making war on anyone. But in 149 B.C., the Numidians, an African people, attacked Carthage, which had no choice but to defend itself. Roman conservatives, spurred on by Cato, jumped at this chance to attack their old enemy. Rome beseiged Carthage for two years and finally, Scipio Aemilianus, adopted grandson of Scipio Africanus, captured the city. In 146 B.C., the same year Rome destroyed Corinth, Scipio received an order to wipe Carthage from the face of the earth. The Romans killed most of the inhabitants, enslaved the others, burned the city, and then plowed over the whole site with earth and salt. Scipio and his friend Polybius stood on a hill and watched Carthage burn. Of this fateful moment, Polybius later wrote:

> At the sight of the city utterly perishing amid the flames, Scipio . . . burst into

The siege of Carthage, 146 B.C., culminated in six days of savage house-to-house fighting.

> tears and stood long reflecting on the inevitable change which awaits cities, nations and dynasties, one and all. . . . This, he thought, had befallen Troy . . . and the once mighty empires of the Assyrians . . . Persians, and that of Macedonia, lately so splendid. . . . And then turning round to a friend who stood near him, he grasped his hand and said: "It is a wonderful sight, but . . . I feel a terror and dread lest someone should one day give the same order about my own native city."[42]

Thus, as one of the world's greatest cities vanished forever, Scipio correctly foretold that its destroyer, Rome, would someday meet a similar fate.

5 Troubles of the Mighty: The Struggle to Maintain Order

In the year 146 B.C. Rome's domain grew substantially. After the destruction of Corinth, all of Greece and parts of Asia Minor came under direct Roman rule. When Rome annihilated Carthage in the same year, northern Africa became a Roman province, too. Although Egypt and most Middle Eastern lands were not yet Roman provinces, they were vassal states that gave Rome allegiance and support. Having amassed tremendous strength and influence, Rome was now the strongest military and political power in the known world.

But the Romans soon learned that administering such a large territory was no easy task. Their constitution and government had originally been designed to rule a single city-state inhabited by one people. They found that this system did not work as well on the scale of a vast collection of nations composed of many different peoples. As a result, in the late second century and early first century B.C., Rome experienced both internal and external troubles as it struggled to maintain order both in Italy and abroad. At home the acquisition of new wealth began to have corruptive effects. Power struggles raged between the patricians and equestrians in Rome as each sought to control the government. Abroad, the main problem was the army. To be effective, it had to be large and commanded by strong generals. But over time Rome's armies had become more loyal to powerful generals than to the state. In their bids for power, these generals brought civil war and political repression that threatened to destroy the republic the Romans had worked so long and hard to build.

Political Corruption Spreads

The troubles of the mightiest Romans during this period were most evident in Rome and its surrounding countryside. The patricians had monopolized political power for centuries, using their system of patronage to control the Senate. In the early second century wealthy patrician families had bought most of the land in the countryside to create the *latifundia*. So a small elite and very conservative group controlled both the government and the land. Now this group felt threatened by the growing power of the equestrian order. These well-to-do commercial and financial leaders demanded a stronger say in government and challenged patrician domination of political affairs.

Many patricians and equestrians had become extremely wealthy. They had also become arrogant and self-indulgent, and felt themselves superior to the masses of "common" poor people. But the wealthy groups recognized that, in order to maintain power and order, it was important to have the support of the commoners. Therefore, both patricians and equestrians frequently appealed to mobs of poor people in Rome and other cities to support their respective positions. Because these commoners had the right to vote in the Popular Assembly, they often became the political tools of the powerful. Elections became marred by open bribery and even violence as patricians and equestrians used their money to sway the results. The honesty, restraint, and self-discipline displayed by earlier generations of Romans, both rich and poor, had begun to erode.

The tribune Tiberius Gracchus (163–133 B.C.), whose radical land redistribution proposals led to rioting.

An Attempt to Restore Fairness

Some Romans were disturbed by the corruption that wealth had brought to Rome. They wanted to restore the dignity and fairness of the political and economic system by narrowing the huge gap between rich and poor. One of these concerned individuals was Tiberius Gracchus, a young man from a well-to-do family, who was elected tribune in 133 B.C. Enthusiastic and well meaning, he immediately proposed a new law that would restore all public land to the state. The state would then have to redistribute the land fairly among the people, both rich and poor, and limit the amount of land any one person could own. According to Plutarch, in advocating passage of the law, Tiberius pleaded:

"The savage beasts in Italy have their particular dens, they have their places of . . . refuge; but the men who bear arms, and expose their lives for the safety of their country, enjoy . . . nothing more in it but the air and light; and, having no houses or settlements of their own, are constrained [forced] to wander from place to place with their wives and children." He told them that . . . they [the commoners] fought indeed and were slain, but it was to maintain the luxury and the wealth of other men. They were styled the masters of the world, but in the meantime had not one foot of ground which they could call their own.[43]

The proposed law became controversial, and it was hotly debated in both the Senate and the streets. Fearing they would lose land and wealth if it passed, some patrician senators persuaded one of the tribunes to veto it. Because all of the tribunes had to consent to any new legislation, the

law was defeated. Tiberius was so deter-
mined to pass the law that he resorted to
unconstitutional means. He quickly pushed
a resolution through the Popular Assembly
that threw out of office the tribune who
had vetoed the land law. Tension gripped
the city as some people sided with Tiberius
and called him a patriot, while others de-
nounced him as a traitor with no respect
for Roman law. Capitalizing on the city's
volatile mood, a group of conservative senators ran into the streets and stirred up a
riot against Tiberius. The members of the
crowd, wrote Plutarch,

> had furnished themselves with clubs
> and staves [wooden poles] from their
> houses, and they themselves picked up
> the feet and other fragments of stools
> and chairs. . . . Thus armed, they made
> towards Tiberius, knocking down those
> whom they found in front of him. . . .
> Tiberius tried to save himself by flight.
> As he was running, he was stopped by
> one who caught hold of him by the
> gown. . . . And stumbling over those
> who before had been knocked down,
> as he was endeavoring to get up again,
> a tribune, one of his colleagues, was
> observed to give him the first fatal
> stroke, by hitting him on the head with
> the foot of a stool.[44]

Ideas Ahead of Their Time

Tiberius died of his wounds, and it seemed
to many in Rome that his proposed reforms had died with him. But ten years
later, in 123 B.C., his brother Gaius Gracchus became a tribune and also devoted

*Gaius Gracchus, whose distribution of corn to the
poor at half price or less marked the beginning of
the Roman welfare system.*

himself to bringing about reform. Gaius,
like his brother, proposed that many public lands be divided among the poorest citizens. Gaius also proposed other radical
changes. For example, he suggested giving
the same voting rights and citizenship priv-
ileges enjoyed in the city of Rome to all
free adult males in Italy, no matter what
their ethnic or tribal backgrounds. In addition, he called for lowering the price of
corn so that more poor people could afford to buy it.

Because they were so controversial at
the time, most of these reforms did not
pass. Opposition to the citizenship law was
especially strong. This was because most

The Citizenship Law Defeated

When Gaius Grac-chus proposed a law granting all free adult males in Italy com-plete Roman citizen-ship, he met with fierce opposition, espe-cially from conserva-tive senators. These senators considered non-Latin Italians to be inferior and unworthy of citizen-ship. Describing the controversial circum-stances surrounding the proposed law, the Roman historian Appian wrote in his Roman History:

"[Gaius Gracchus] called on the Latin allies to demand the full rights of Roman citizenship, since the Senate could not with decency refuse this privilege to men of the same race. To the other allies, who were not allowed to vote in Roman elections, he sought to give the right of suffrage [the right to vote], in order to have their help in the enactment of laws which he had in [mind]. The Sen-ate was very much alarmed at this, and it ordered the consuls to give the following public notice, 'Nobody who does not possess the right of suffrage shall stay in the city or approach within forty stades [about five miles] of it while voting is going on concerning these laws.' The Sen-ate also persuaded Livius Drusus, another tribune, to . . . vote against the laws proposed by Gracchus, but not to tell the people his reasons for doing so; for a tribune was not required to give reasons for his veto; in order to con-ciliate [win the favor of] the people they gave Drusus the privilege of founding twelve colonies, and the plebeians were so much pleased with this that they scoffed at the laws proposed by Gracchus."

native Romans still held strong prejudices against people descended from ancient enemies like the Samnites and Gauls. On the day that the law was to be voted upon, opponents started violent street riots just as they had done ten years before. Gaius was murdered and his body thrown into the Tiber.

The Gracchi brothers had courageously but vainly attempted to restore fairness and order to the Roman political system. But their proposals were simply ahead of their time. Though the brothers themselves had failed, the ideas they championed lived

on, and in time the Romans adopted many of the reforms. For instance, Rome granted citizenship to all free adult males in Italy south of the Po valley in 88 B.C., some thirty-five years after Gaius's death. Even-tually, the Gracchi brothers were re-membered as heroes. The people, said Plutarch, "ordered their statues to be made and set up in public view; they conse-crated [made into shrines] the places where they were slain. . . . Many came . . . thither to their devotions [prayers], and daily worshipped there, as at the temple of the gods."[45]

Marius's Reforms

While Rome struggled with domestic affairs and reforms in the late second century B.C., it also had trouble governing its many, diverse, and often faraway provinces. One problem was that many of the provincial governors lacked the administrative skills to run these territories efficiently. Although some able governors were appointed, as a rule they served for only one year. Because they had to spend so much time getting used to their posts, many of the important aspects of provincial government fell into the hands of inexperienced native officials. Also, tax collection in most provinces was corrupt, and much of the money collected ended up in the pockets of tax collectors or local officials instead of paying for government services.

Another problem in governing the empire was raising enough well-trained troops to guard and police the provinces. Throughout most of the second century B.C., Rome had maintained its long-standing tradition of allowing only landowners to serve in the army. But as wealthy Romans bought up most of the small farms to create *latifundia*, the number of landowners decreased sharply. Therefore, by the end of the century, it had become difficult to raise enough troops for the many garrisons needed in the provinces. Having a smaller army was potentially dangerous for Rome, because conquered peoples sometimes rebelled, and new enemies periodically threatened the empire's borders.

A popular general named Gaius Marius solved this problem after he became consul in 107 B.C. Marius eliminated the landownership qualification for military service and allowed any Roman citizen to serve. He increased wages and gave all soldiers the same weapons and training, creating a new professional army much larger and effective than the old one. According to Plutarch:

> [Marius] disciplined and trained them, giving them practice in long marches, and running of every sort,

Marius inspecting his troops. The soldier beside him, known as an aquilifer, *carries the* aquila, *the silver eagle signifying Roman power.*

Deeds Nobler than Words

Marius was an able soldier and leader. The following excerpt is from a speech, recorded by the Roman historian Sallust, and taken from Latin Literature in Translation, *that Marius made to a group of commoners after being elected consul in 107 B.C. Pointing out that a person's deeds, not the circumstances of birth, make the person noble, Marius said:*

"Compare, now, my fellow-citizens, me, who am a *new man,* with those haughty nobles. What they have but heard or read, I have witnessed or performed. What they have learned from books, I have acquired in the field; and whether deeds or words are of greater estimation, it is for you to consider. They despise my humbleness of birth; I condemn their imbecility. . . . The circumstance of birth, indeed, I consider as one and the same to all; but think that he who best exerts himself is the noblest. . . . If the patricians justly despise me, let them also despise their own ancestors, whose nobility, like mine, had its origin in merit. They envy me the honor that I have received; let them also envy me the toils, the abstinence [going without comforts], and the perils, by which I obtained that honor. But they, men eaten up with pride, live as if they disdained all the distinctions [honors] that you can bestow, and yet sue [ask] for those distinctions as if they had lived so as to merit them."

Gaius Marius (c. 155–86 B.C.) served as consul seven times between 107 and 86 B.C.

and compelling every man to carry his own baggage and prepare his own food. . . . Thenceforward [after that] laborious soldiers, who did their work silently without grumbling, had the name of "Marius's mules."[46]

Marius also reorganized the army. He reduced the number of men in a century from one hundred to eighty and created a new unit called a cohort, consisting of from six to ten centuries. Each legion had ten cohorts for a total of about five thousand men. Military camp life became organized and disciplined. As Polybius described a standard camp:

> The whole camp . . . forms a square, and the way in which the streets are laid out and its general arrangement give it the appearance of a town. . . . As everyone knows exactly in which street his tent will be . . . [each soldier entering camp] goes straight on . . . and reaches his own house without fail, as he knows both the quarter and the exact spot where his residence is situated.[47]

Military commanders kept strict discipline and punished rule breakers harshly. Said Polybius:

> The bastinado [beating with sticks and stones] is . . . inflicted on those who steal anything from the camp; on those who give false evidence . . . and finally on anyone who has been punished thrice [three times] for the same fault.[48]

As a result of Marius's reforms, the Roman army became the effective defensive and offensive tool that Rome needed to protect and enforce the rules of its empire.

In the Hands of a Few Ambitious Men

Although Marius had strengthened the army and the empire, he had also created a problem that Rome had not previously encountered. Most of the soldiers were now volunteers and career men who looked forward to getting pensions or parcels of land when they retired. Because the state did not provide such allowances, to acquire them a soldier had to depend on his general's influence with wealthy Romans. In time, the troops tended to become more loyal to their generals than to the state. This opened the way for ambitious and popular generals to use their armies to oppose the government and even to march on Rome itself.

Marius himself became involved in the first such challenge to state power. For years he remained the most powerful and popular Roman general, but in 88 B.C. his former assistant, a general named Sulla, became consul and challenged his position. Both men won large groups of supporters in Rome. Marius, who had been born a commoner, declared himself the champion of the plebeians, while Sulla, an aristocrat, gained the backing of the patricians and

Sulla (138–78 B.C.), an aristocrat and conservative politician, wanted wealthy patricians to control the Senate and other institutions.

Sulla's Reign of Terror

After winning the civil war that erupted when he marched on Rome, Sulla began proscribing, or condemning to death, his political enemies. In his Life of Sulla, *Plutarch described how on the first day of the massacres, Sulla cruelly*

"proscribed eighty persons, and . . . after one day's respite [pause], he posted two hundred and twenty more, and on the third, again as many. In an address to the people on this occasion, he told them that he had put as many names as he could think of; those which had escaped his memory, he would publish at a future time. He issued an edict likewise, making death the punishment of humanity, proscribing any who should dare to . . . [protect] a proscribed person without exception to brother, son, or parents. And to him who should slay any one proscribed person, he ordained two talents [a sum of money] reward, even were it a slave who had killed his master, or a son his father. And what was thought most unjust of all, he caused the attainder [guilt of the proscribed] to pass upon their sons, and sons' sons, and made open sale of all their property."

Sulla's list of proscribed enemies hangs in the Forum. He killed and seized the property of forty senators and 1,600 other well-to-do Romans.

Sulla leads his troops in battle. Among his victories was one over King Mithridates of Pontus, a kingdom in northern Asia Minor.

the Senate. Shortly after becoming consul, Sulla left Rome to put down a rebellion in Asia Minor. With Sulla gone, Marius took control of the Roman state and murdered many of Sulla's followers. Soon afterward, Marius died, but his supporters remained in power. In 83 B.C. Sulla returned from the east and marched on Rome, becoming the first Roman general to attack the city's established government. A brief but bloody civil war ensued, after which Sulla had himself appointed dictator in 82 B.C.

Sulla's rule was harsh. He immediately murdered many of Marius's supporters and their families. "Men were butchered in the embraces of their wives," recalled Plutarch, "children in the arms of their mothers."[49] Sulla also killed a number of wealthy people on trumped-up charges, confiscated their money, and distributed it to his troops in order to keep the soldiers' loyalty. Wrote Plutarch:

> Those who perished through public animosity [political opposition] . . . were nothing in comparison to the numbers of those who suffered for their riches. Even the murderers

began to say, that "his fine house killed this man, a garden that [man], a third, his hot baths."[50]

Next, Sulla forced several governmental changes. He increased the power of the patrician senators, while decreasing the power of the equestrians, both in the Senate and other areas of government. He also greatly restricted the powers of the tribunes.

Sulla retired and died in 78 B.C. Most of the changes he made did not last long. Within a decade the government's power structure had largely returned to the way it was before he took power. But the civil war and Sulla's reign had a more lasting effect in one important way. They showed that the Roman government was no longer strong enough to maintain order, while the army clearly was. Rome now entered an era in which military strongmen, under the pretext of providing order and stability, would wield the power of empire. The whims and ambitions of a few powerful men would begin to overshadow and threaten the republican government that Rome had established more than four centuries before.

Chapter

6 Fighting Slaves and Pirates: Strongmen Vie for Power

The power struggle between Marius and Sulla set a precedent in Rome. In the two decades following Sulla's death in 78 B.C., strong military leaders, some of whom were also wealthy aristocrats, repeatedly manipulated the government and the public in order to further their own careers. Foremost among the strongmen in this period were Pompey and Crassus. Both rose to power by saving the state from serious dangers, specifically rebellious Roman generals, slave uprisings, and pirates. Of these dangers, the Roman public found the slave uprisings the most frightening. The number of slaves in the republic, especially in Italy, had grown tremendously over the centuries and a constant and real threat existed that slaves might turn on their masters.

For Pompey and Crassus, the military campaigns against the slaves and others were less patriotic endeavors than they were opportunities to build up their own prestige and power. While the two men exploited these situations, they became rivals for the support of the people and control of the government. During these years only one influential man—the politician and orator Cicero—openly opposed the generals and fought to maintain the integrity of the republic. But without the backing of the army, he was no match for the power of men like Pompey and Crassus.

Pompey and Crassus Rise to Prominence

Pompey was the first military leader to attempt to fill the power vacuum left when Sulla died. One of Sulla's most trusted subordinates, Pompey won a number of battles

Gnaeus Pompey (106–48 B.C.), often called "the Great," was one of Rome's most popular war heroes.

Pompey rides in a triumph, or victory parade, celebrating one of his successful military campaigns.

who then assumed command of the rebellious army. Pompey soundly defeated Perperna and returned triumphant to Rome in 71 B.C.

While Pompey was acquiring glory and power in Spain, Crassus gained prominence in Italy. Crassus, who was six years older than Pompey, was an aristocrat and the wealthiest man in Rome, possessing silver mines and vast tracts of real estate. Like Pompey, he had been one of Sulla's loyal officers during the civil war. After Sulla's death, Crassus went back to managing his business affairs and waited for a situation to arise that would allow him to take command of an army.

Crassus's chance came in 73 B.C., when a group of slaves at a gladiator school in

The Thracian slave Spartacus, whose rebellion the Romans called the Servile War.

against Marius's supporters during the civil war. Only in his midtwenties at the time, Pompey earned a reputation as a daring and able soldier and became popular with Sulla's supporters in the Senate and upper classes.

In 77 B.C. the Senate gave Pompey an important assignment. His job was to take an army to Spain and put down a rebellion led by a Roman general named Quintus Sertorius. Sertorius, a supporter of Marius, had repeatedly defeated Sulla's forces in Spain between 80 and 78 B.C. In the following year Sertorius had managed to take control of large sections of Spain and was still openly defying the Roman government. Pompey took forty thousand troops to Spain and opposed Sertorius for five years. In 72 B.C. Sertorius was assassinated by one of his own supporters, Perperna,

Capua, about one hundred miles south of Rome, escaped and terrorized the surrounding countryside. They were led by a slave named Spartacus. Plutarch recalled that seventy-eight of the slaves

> got out of a cook's shop chopping-knives and spits, and made their way through the city, and lighting by the way on several wagons that were carrying gladiators' arms to another city, they seized upon them and armed themselves. And seizing upon a defensible place, they chose three captains, of whom Spartacus was chief . . . a man not only of high spirit and valiant, but in understanding, also, and in gentleness superior to his condition.[51]

Spartacus freed many slaves in central Italy, built a formidable slave army, and

Roman slaves awaiting sale at a slave market. Each wore a sign around the neck describing his or her qualities.

defeated several small Roman armies sent to put down the uprising. Eventually the Senate dispatched armies under the consuls Gellius and Lentulus, but Spartacus defeated them, too. The government was now fearful and desperate. Realizing that the most popular and able general of the day, Pompey, was busy in Spain, Crassus seized the opportunity and offered to put down the rebellious slaves.

Roman Slaves

Crassus soon found that he had taken on a formidable task. Tens of thousands of slaves had eagerly turned on their masters and joined the slave army. This army was growing daily, and Spartacus was giving many of the slaves gladiator training, making them more than a match for Roman troops. The fact that Spartacus's rebellion was so large and initially successful was a sign that the institution of slavery had become one of Rome's greatest weaknesses. The large number of discontented people living in servitude posed a constant threat to free Romans. At the time of Spartacus's revolt, perhaps nearly one-fifth of Italy's population of about 5 million people were slaves. In Rome itself, about 200,000 of the city's 1 million inhabitants were slaves.

Slavery had not always been so widespread in Rome. In the days of the kings and early republic, most citizens were small farmers who did most of their work themselves. There was little need for slaves, who, as historian Will Durant explained,

> had been costly and few, and therefore had been treated with consideration as

valuable members of the family. In the sixth century B.C., when Rome began her career of conquest [in Italy], war captives were sold in rising number to the aristocracy, the business classes, and even to plebeians; and the status of the slave sank. Legally he could be dealt with as any other piece of property.[52]

The number of slaves steadily increased, especially during and after the third century B.C., when Rome began conquering foreign peoples. In time, Roman slaves were not only of Italian stock, but also of Greek, Syrian, Numidian, Gallic, and Iberian descent.

Slavery negatively affected the lives of slaves and free Romans alike. The slaves, lacking freedom and working long hours to enrich their masters' lives rather than their own, had little or no self-esteem. Some slaves were well treated, but many were routinely beaten or even killed by their masters. As Frank Cowell pointed out, slavery also

proved to be a great evil to the free Romans. . . . Rich Romans . . . owning perhaps hundreds of slaves, employed them for every conceivable household task and for most manufacturing and industrial jobs: spinning, weaving, baking, brewing, shoe-making, book-copying, and so on. . . . [The Romans] profited to the extent that they did not have to do such jobs themselves. But neither were they able to employ free laborers for such work. Consequently a race of independent craftsmen and manufacturers were deprived of work. . . . In more ways than one, therefore, Roman society and Roman life were weakened and impoverished by the huge slave colony in their midst.[53]

With such a large proportion of Romans living in the misery of human bondage, slave rebellions were perhaps inevitable. Several such rebellions occurred in the second century B.C. The largest was a revolt in Sicily led by a slave named Ennus, who gathered some twenty thousand followers in 134 B.C. and set up his own small kingdom. It took a large Roman army two years to put down the uprising.

Spartacus's Defeat

But even Ennus's revolt was small compared to that of Spartacus. By the time Crassus fielded an army against him in 72 B.C., Spartacus's own army had swelled to at least ninety thousand, most of them well armed and well trained. Many Romans feared that Spartacus might free every slave in Italy and then march on Rome. Crassus realized that he had a golden opportunity. If he could defeat Spartacus, he would be the greatest hero of the day and gain tremendous prestige and power.

At first Crassus did not fare well. He ordered one of his officers to take two legions, follow Spartacus, and observe the slave army. But the officer became overconfident, attacked the slaves, and was badly defeated. Crassus then received more bad news. Pompey was winding up his Spanish campaign and would be returning to Italy to help fight the slaves. To ensure that he himself would get all the credit for defeating Spartacus, Crassus desperately tried to provoke a major battle with the slaves before Pompey arrived.

Crassus caught up with Spartacus in 71 B.C. in the southern Italian province of Lucania. The two armies formed ranks and

Breeding Slaves

The worst slave owners treated their slaves like animals to be bred and sold. The Roman Cato was such an owner. In his work On Agriculture, *he described the best ways to keep, breed, and make a profit from slaves. This made an impression on many Romans, including Plutarch, who later wrote:*

"When at home, a slave had to be either at work or asleep. Indeed Cato greatly favored the sleepy ones, accounting them more docile than those who were wakeful, and more fit for anything when refreshed with slumber than those who lacked it. Being also of the opinion that the greater cause of misbehavior in slaves was their sexual passions, he arranged for the males to consort [have sex] with the females at a fixed price and permitted none to approach a woman outside the household. . . . He also lent money to those of his slaves who wished it; they would buy boys and, after training them and teaching them at Cato's expense, would sell them again after a year. Many of these Cato would keep for himself, crediting the trainer slave with the price offered by the highest bidder."

Cato's writings about slavery were widely read in his day.

Spartacus dies in battle. His courageous fight for freedom was later immortalized in popular paintings, novels, and films.

faced each other in an open field. Spartacus, wrote Plutarch, stood beside his horse in full view of his troops and

> drew out his sword and killed him [the horse], saying, if he got [won] the day he should have a great many better horses of the enemies', and if he lost it he should have no need of this. And so making directly towards Crassus himself, through the midst of arms and wounds, he missed him, but slew two centurions who fell upon him together. At last being deserted by those that were about him, he himself stood his ground, and, surrounded by the enemy, bravely defending himself, was cut to pieces.[54]

Most of the slaves were killed, although some escaped and tried to regroup. Unfortunately for Crassus, Pompey arrived soon afterward, tracked down and defeated the fugitives, and thereby shared in the victory. As an example to other slaves, the six thousand survivors of Spartacus's army were crucified along the road to Rome.

Pompey and the Pirates

The defeat of Spartacus brought Crassus and Pompey the complete allegiance of the army and great popularity with the public. The two men easily won election as consuls in 70 B.C. But unlike the situation in previous centuries, when the consuls largely did the Senate's bidding, Crassus and Pompey used their power and prestige to control the government. To maintain their popularity with the people, they restored the tribunes' powers, which Sulla had stripped. Crassus and Pompey also expelled many of the senators Sulla had put in office. In the next few years few Romans dared to challenge either Pompey, Crassus, or Crassus's right-hand man, a young army officer named Julius Caesar.

In the decade following their election as consuls, Pompey and Crassus remained the most powerful men in Rome. Each constantly sought whatever means possible to increase his public popularity and military standing. Pompey was more successful,

A Rebellion "Not Unreasonable"

Before Spartacus's revolt the largest slave rebellion in Rome had been the Sicilian uprising of 134 B.C. led by Ennus. In his fascinating work, Library of History, *the Roman historian Diodorus wrote about the causes of the rebellion. Diodorus showed sympathy for the plight of the Sicilian slaves, an indication that not all Romans believed in treating slaves cruelly. Diodorus wrote:*

"Never had there been such an uprising of slaves as now occurred in Sicily. In it many cities experienced terrible misfortunes, and untold numbers of men, woman and children suffered most grievous calamities; and the whole island was on the point of falling into the power of the runaways. . . . To most people these events came to pass unlooked for, and unexpectedly; but to men of competent political judgement their occurrence did not seem unreasonable. . . . The Slave War broke out from the following cause. The Sicilians, being grown very rich and elegant in their manner of living, bought up large numbers of slaves. They bought them in droves [great numbers] from the places where they were reared [bred], and immediately branded them with marks on their bodies. . . . Oppressed by the grinding toil and beatings, maltreated for the most part beyond all reason, the slaves could endure it no longer. Therefore, meeting together at suitable opportunities they discussed revolt, until at last they put their plan into effect."

executing one brilliant military campaign after another. His most famous exploits were against fleets of pirates, who for some time had been terrorizing the Mediterranean and interfering with trade and commerce. According to Plutarch:

> The power of the pirates . . . gained life and boldness. . . . They had diverse arsenals, or piratic harbors, as likewise watchtowers and beacons, all along the sea-coast; and [pirate] fleets were here received that were well-manned with the finest mariners, and well-served with the expertest pilots, and

The six thousand survivors of Spartacus's army are crucified along the Via Appia.

A Monster Breathing Wickedness

When Cicero, by the brilliance of his oratory, exposed Catiline's plot to overthrow Rome's government, the Senate declared Catiline an enemy of the people. Catiline then fled the city, confirming his guilt. One of Cicero's subsequent speeches against Catiline, quoted in The Ancient World to 300 A.D., *colorfully and dramatically celebrated the expulsion of the would-be tyrant:*

"At length, O Romans, we have dismissed from the city, or driven out or, when he was departing of his own accord, we have pursued with words, Lucius Catiline, mad with audacity [arrogance], breathing wickedness, impiously planning mischief to his country, threatening fire and sword to you and to his city. He is gone, he has departed, he has disappeared, he has rushed out. No injury will now be prepared against these walls within the walls themselves by that monster and progeny [offspring] of wickedness. And we have without controversy defeated him, the sole general of this domestic war. . . . Beyond all question we ruin the man; we have defeated him splendidly when we have driven him from secret treachery into open warfare. But that he has not taken with him his sword red with blood as he intended—that he has left us alive—that we wrested the weapon from his hands— that he has left the citizens safe and the city standing, what great and overwhelming grief must you think that this is to him! Now he lies prostrate [humbled], O Romans, and feels himself stricken down . . . and often casts back his eyes towards this city, which he mourns over as snatched from his jaws, but which seems to me to rejoice at having vomited forth such a pest and cast it out of doors."

composed of swift-sailing and light-built vessels adapted for their special purpose. . . . This piratic power having got dominion and control of all the Mediterranean, there was no place left for navigation and commerce. And this it was which . . . made the Romans . . . determine at last to send out Pompey to recover the seas from the pirates.[55]

For his campaign against the pirates, Pompey received five hundred ships and complete authority over the entire Mediterranean Sea. The government also gave him control of all coastal lands for a distance of fifty miles inland. No other Roman general had ever before been granted absolute power over so much territory. Pompey used this extraordinary power to his best advantage. In 67 B.C., in a brilliant, lightning-fast operation, he cleared the seas of pirates in a mere forty days. He sank or burned thirteen hundred pirate ships and captured another four hundred, all without losing a single Roman ship. This incredible achievement made Pompey a hero of epic proportions. Meanwhile, the envious Crassus, though lacking exploits to match Pompey's, managed to hold on to his own power and popularity in Rome.

The Whims of Powerful Men

But great as it was, Crassus's and Pompey's power did not go completely unchallenged during these years. In the midsixties B.C. Cicero, an equestrian who had become the most famous defense lawyer of the era, gained much popularity with the people. During the consular election in 63 B.C., he dared to oppose the candidates supported by Crassus and Caesar. Cicero won and immediately declared himself the champion of the common people against Crassus and his aristocratic supporters. Cicero also championed the republic itself, often arguing that it had become a corrupt tool in the hands of a few greedy men. "Cicero really tried to maintain the inherited system of Roman government," wrote Chester Starr, "and dreamed of uniting the senatorial and equestrian classes in its support."[56]

Cicero's most dramatic accomplishment was saving the republic from a military takeover. In 63 B.C. hearing that Lucius Catiline, a patrician and former colleague of Crassus, was plotting to kill the consuls and seize the government, Cicero acted swiftly. In a series of powerful speeches, Cicero convinced the Senate to grant him and his fellow consul Antonius whatever powers necessary to foil the plot. In January 62 B.C. Antonius attacked and defeated the small army Catiline was raising, killing Catiline in the process. Meanwhile, Cicero arrested Catiline's supporters in Rome and ordered their immediate execution. The rescue of the government increased Cicero's prestige, but he lacked the army's backing, which Pompey and Crassus enjoyed. So Cicero never managed to gain the power necessary to eliminate these strongmen and restore the government to its former position of authority.

To Cicero's distress the subordination of the state to the whims of powerful men only grew worse. Late in 62 B.C., word came that Pompey, who had just finished some successful military exploits in the eastern empire, was returning to Italy. Many people, including Crassus, feared that Pompey would march his army on Rome as Sulla had. As Plutarch told it:

> Rumors of every kind were scattered abroad about Pompey . . . so that there was a great tumult and stir, as if he designed . . . to march with his army into the city and establish himself securely as sole ruler. Crassus withdrew himself, together with his children and property, out of the city.[57]

But to everyone's surprise, Pompey disbanded his army and rode into Rome accompanied by only a few close friends. This was a shrewd move. By passing up this chance to become a dictator, Pompey made himself more popular than ever with the common people. This, he believed, would improve his chances of later seizing power with the benefit of widespread public support.

"The Interests of the State Will Unite Us"

The only power-hungry general that Cicero respected was Pompey. Probably Cicero felt that Pompey's exploits outweighed his personal ambitions. In the following correspondence taken from Latin Literature in Translation, *the orator greeted the general, who was off fighting a war at the time. Cicero referred to his own exploit, the exposure of Catiline's plot, and offered to support Pompey on his return to Rome.*

"Marcus Tullius Cicero, son of Marcus, greets Gnaeus Pompey, son of Gnaeus, Imperator or Supreme Commander.

If you and the army are well, all is well. From your official despatch I, along with all other people, have received the greatest pleasure; for you have held out to us that high hope of peace, which I was guaranteeing to all in reliance upon you. . . . Although your personal letter to me gave me only a slight indication of your affection toward me, yet I want you to know that it was pleasing; for there is nothing in which I am wont [inclined] to rejoice so much as in the consciousness of services done to my friends. . . . Doubtless the interests of the state will bring us together and unite us, if my great zeal towards you fails to do so. . . . I want you to know . . . that what I have done for the salvation of our native land is approved by the judgment and testimony of the wide, wide world. Upon your return here, you will realize that my achievements are the result of such prudence and magnitude [caution and greatness] of mind, that you, a much greater man than [Scipio] Africanus, will be glad to have me . . . united with you publicly and privately."

For a while it appeared that Crassus and Pompey would once more become rivals for power in Rome. However, in 60 B.C. Julius Caesar returned from Spain, where he had served for a year and gained fame and prestige as a general and administrator. Caesar, now nearly as powerful a figure in Rome as Pompey and Crassus, sought the office of consul. Rather than become involved in the power struggle between these men, Caesar wisely chose to create a coalition. He made a secret pact in which Crassus and Pompey promised to join forces with Caesar, help get him elected consul, and then rule Rome with him. This coalition of three later became known as the First Triumvirate. At first the plan went as scheduled, and Caesar won election as consul in 59 B.C. At the time, Crassus and Pompey could not foresee that, in a meteoric rise to power, their colleague would sweep them aside and bring the republic to its knees.

Chapter

7 Caesar's Exploits: The Republic in Peril

The formation of a triumvirate by Caesar, Pompey, and Crassus was the strongest challenge yet to the integrity of the Roman Republic. Each of these men enjoyed varying amounts of control over or popularity with the army, the Senate, the wealthy classes, and the common people. By combining their considerable powers and influences, the leaders were able to intimidate and overshadow every governmental body and office. Though the fact was never stated officially, in effect Rome was now a dictatorship of three.

Early Roman senators listen to a speech by a foreign ambassador.

Julius Caesar (c. 100–44 B.C.), whose ruthless bid for power threatened Rome's traditional republican government.

But the triumvirate, though impressive as a political force, was inherently unstable. Each triumvir was an ambitious, selfish man whose ultimate plans did not include sharing power with the other two. In time the three-way alliance would shatter, igniting disruptive civil war and opening the way for one of the triumvirs to seize power as a single dictator.

Rule by Terror

After his election as consul in 59 B.C., Julius Caesar immediately asserted the triumvirate's awesome power. Caesar proposed a law that would distribute state-owned lands among Pompey's veteran soldiers. When the tribunes, many senators, and the other consul, Bibulus, all opposed the law, the triumvirs used strong-arm tactics to get their way. Caesar's and Pompey's henchmen chased political opponents away from the Senate and other public buildings. They beat up Cato the Younger, the leader of the opposition, and so intimidated Bibulus that out of fear he remained in his house for most of his term as consul. Because of Caesar's illegal rule by terrorism, the land law and many other laws favorable to the triumvirs passed.

Cicero's remained the only important republican voice left. He bravely argued that the Roman government had not been founded by and for a few individuals, but was the result of generations of Romans working together for the common good. "Our state," he said,

> was the result not of one man's genius but of many men's, not of one man's life but of several centuries and periods. . . . [Even] if genius were concentrated in one man, he could [not] have such foresight as to embrace everything at any one moment; actual experience stretching over the ages is needed.[58]

Cicero blamed the current state of affairs on the steady decay of Roman values that wealth and greed had brought in the preceding two centuries. He stated, "It is due to our own moral failure and not to

Marcus Tullius Cicero (106–43 B.C.), senator, writer, and patriot, defended the republic in the first century B.C.

any accident of chance that, while retaining the name, we have lost the reality of a republic."[59] Cicero called upon all Roman leaders, most especially the triumvirs, to recognize their duty to the state and to the people, saying:

> These men of whom I have spoken, who guide the ship of state—on what objective must they fasten their gaze and set their course? Their objective must be that which . . . can satisfy the earnest wishes of all men of good sense, of substance, and of loyalty—I mean, a settled and honorable security [of traditional rights]. Those who aim at the end indeed belong to the party of patriots; those who further it show their high merit and are justly held to be the backbone of their country.[60]

Caesar's Dishonesty

Most Romans knew Julius Caesar as ambitious and ruthless. His outright dishonesty was also well known. For example, in his biography of Caesar, the historian Suetonius wrote:

"He was not particularly honest in money matters, either while as provincial governor or while holding office at Rome. Several memoirs record that as Governor-General of Western Spain he not only begged his allies for money to settle his debts, but wantonly sacked several . . . towns, though they had accepted his terms and opened their gates to welcome him. In Gaul he plundered large and small temples . . . and more often gave towns over to pillage [looting] because their inhabitants were rich than because they had offended him. As a result he collected larger quantities of gold than he could handle, and began selling it for silver, in Italy and the provinces, at 750 denarii to the pound—which was about two-thirds of the official exchange rate. In the course of his first consulship he stole 3,000 lb of gold from the Capitol, and replaced it with the same weight of gilded bronze. He sold alliances and thrones for cash, making King Ptolemy XII of Egypt give him and Pompey nearly 1,500,000 gold pieces; and later paid his Civil War army, and the expenses of his triumphs and entertainments, by open extortion [obtaining money through threats] and sacrilege [theft of temple money]."

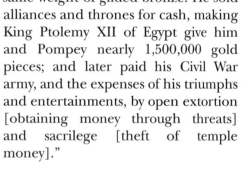

Julius Caesar as he appeared shortly before his death. In response to his critics, he said, "I have always put the good name and honor of the state first."

But these words fell on deaf ears. Caesar and the other triumvirs continued to intimidate the government. What is more, to get rid of Cicero they accused him of abusing his former consular powers by executing Catiline's followers without trials. To avoid certain conviction and death, Cicero went into hiding in Greece.

The Conquest of Gaul

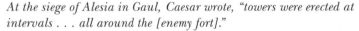

Caesar's term as consul ended in 58 B.C., but through their connections and influence the triumvirs continued to hold the real power in Rome for some time to come. For Caesar, however, political power was not enough. He still did not have military experience and backing to match Pompey's. So Caesar used his influence to get himself appointed proconsul, or governor, of the province of Transalpine Gaul, now southern France. His goal was to use the province as a base of operations from which to launch military campaigns northward into Gaul. At the time, Gaul, a non-Roman territory, was an ill-defined area roughly including what later became central and northern France and the Netherlands. The peoples of the region often fought among themselves and with semi-civilized tribes from what is now Germany, as well as with the Romans on their southern borders.

By conquering Gaul, Caesar hoped to gain much. First, he would build a large, battle-hardened army loyal mainly to him. Second, he could use the riches plundered during the conquests to pay his henchmen

At the siege of Alesia in Gaul, Caesar wrote, "towers were erected at intervals . . . all around the [enemy fort]."

in Rome and bribe public officials to vote the way he desired. That way, he could maintain his share of the triumviral power during his absence. Third, he would be defeating an ancient enemy, the Gauls, and expanding the empire, making him immensely popular with the common people. To impress the Roman people with his achievements, Caesar kept a detailed journal describing his exploits. His *Commentaries on the Gallic Wars* remains an informative, fascinating, and exciting account of Roman military life.

During the eight years he spent in Gaul, Caesar accomplished all of his goals and more. By 57 B.C. he had driven deep into northeastern Gaul, and in the following year he subdued the tribes along the Atlantic coast. In 55 B.C. Caesar boldly crossed the strait now known as the English Channel and invaded Britain. Three years later, in 52 B.C., the Gauls rebelled against their new masters, and Caesar met the Gallic armies in a final battle at Alesia, in northeastern Gaul. As Caesar described it, the Gallic cavalry

> filled the plain, which . . . was three miles long. Their infantry was posted a little farther back on some rising ground. . . . I ordered the [Roman] cavalry to ride out of camp and engage the enemy. . . . As the battle was being fought in full view of everyone, so that every brave deed could be seen and no act of cowardice could be hidden, the men on each side were impelled [driven] both for the desire for glory and the fear of disgrace to fight to the utmost of their strength. The battle raged from midday until almost sunset. . . . The enemy could see that I was coming because of the scarlet cloak

which I always wore to mark me out in action. . . . So the enemy rushed into battle. The shout was raised on both sides. . . . Our men dispensed with [stopped using] javelins and got to work with their swords. Suddenly, the Gauls saw our cavalry coming in from the rear; fresh cohorts of infantry were also bearing down. The enemy turned and ran. As they ran the cavalry were upon them. There was a great slaughter. . . . Out of all that great [enemy] army very few got safely back to camp.[61]

During his successful campaigns in Gaul, Caesar built a loyal personal army of thirteen legions, a total of more than fifty thousand troops. He also added huge territories to the empire, bolstering his popularity and political power.

Crossing the Rubicon

While in Gaul, Caesar remained informed of events in Rome. By 50 B.C. the government and parts of the city were in a state of near chaos. In 53 B.C. Crassus had attempted to gain his own military glory by leading a campaign in Syria against the Parthians, a west Asian people once subject to the Seleucid kingdom. Crassus died that year in battle, leaving Pompey the only triumvir left in Rome.

Though he was a skilled general, Pompey was a poor administrator and politician. He stood by and did nothing as rival factions in the government stirred up mobs and riots, and he allowed himself to become a tool of conservative senators. These men sought to destroy the remainder of the triumvirate by pitting Pompey

The Landing in Britain

Caesar's war commentaries are filled with detailed and colorful descriptions of his eight-year conquests of Gaul and Britain. Typical is the following passage from Commentaries *about the first landing on the British coast:*

"After moving on about eight miles, we ran the ships ashore on an open, evenly shelved beach. The natives, however, had realized what we planned to do. They had sent their cavalry and their chariots [a type of weapon which they nearly always used in battle] on ahead. The rest of their troops followed behind, and they now stood ready to oppose our landing. Things were very difficult for us indeed, and for the following reasons. Our ships were too big to run ashore except where the water was deep; the troops knew nothing of the ground on which they were to fight and not only had their hands full but were weighed down by the heavy armor which they carried; they had to jump down from the transports, get a footing in the surf, and fight the enemy all at the same time. The enemy, on the other hand, were quite unencumbered [without heavy armor] and knew the ground well. . . . They hurled their weapons boldly at us and spurred on their horses, which were trained for this sort of fighting. All this had a most disturbing effect on our men. . . . [Eventually] they were able to make use of slings, arrows, and artillery [*tormenta,* or catapults] to drive the enemy back and clear the beach. . . . As our men still hesitated, chiefly because of the depth of the water, the man who carried the eagle [emblem] of the Tenth Legion, after praying to the gods that what he was going to do would bring good luck to the legion, shouted out in a loud voice: 'Come on, men! Jump, unless you want to lose your eagle to the enemy. I, in any case, will do my duty to my country and to my general.' He then threw himself from the ship and began to go toward the enemy, carrying the eagle with him. He was followed by all the rest, who jumped into the sea together, shouting out to each other that they must not disgrace themselves by losing their eagle."

A group of Roman senators try to persuade Pompey to defend Rome against Caesar. Unable to mount a credible defense, Pompey fled the city.

Caesar crosses the Rubicon River, openly defying the government and igniting civil war.

and Caesar against each other. In January 49 B.C. the Senate declared Pompey a protector of the state and Caesar a public enemy. Caesar was ordered to disband his army at once. When Caesar's friend and supporter Mark Antony protested, senators threatened his life and drove him from the city.

Learning of these events, Caesar realized that he had a fateful decision to make. His army was camped along the Rubicon River, the formal boundary between the Po valley, then the province of Cisalpine Gaul, and Italy. If Caesar obeyed the Senate and disbanded his army, his military and political career would be over. On the other hand, if he marched his troops across the river, the Senate would interpret it as an armed attack on the state and order Pompey to retaliate. According to the Roman historian Suetonius, on January 7, 49 B.C., Caesar

> paused for a while, and realizing what a step he was taking, he turned to those about him and said: "Even yet we

may turn back; but once cross yon little bridge, and the whole issue is with the sword. . . . Take we the course which the signs of the gods and the false dealing of our foes point out. The die is cast!"[62]

With these words, Caesar boldly crossed the river and plunged Rome into a new and disastrous civil war.

Pompey's Demise

With Caesar marching toward Rome at the head of his huge army, many people in Rome and its surrounding countryside panicked. Wrote Plutarch:

> The city of Rome was overwhelmed by a rush of people from all the neighboring places. All this caused so much disturbance that those who lived in Rome, seeing such confusion and disorder, began to leave the city as fast as the others came in.[63]

Because of all the fear and confusion, Pompey could not organize a defense fast enough, and he, some of his troops, and many senators fled Italy. Pompey crossed the Adriatic Sea into Greece and began raising an army to oppose Caesar.

Caesar did not pursue Pompey right away. Instead, Caesar wisely took the time to consolidate his own power in Rome and eliminate Pompey's supporters in Italy and Spain. In 48 B.C. Caesar crossed the Adriatic and challenged Pompey. The two Roman armies met at Pharsalus in central Greece. Caesar later wrote:

> Our men, as soon as the signal was given, charged forward . . . at the double, hurled their javelins, and immediately, as they had been instructed to do, drew their swords. Pompey's men stood up to the attack well. They met the javelins with their shields, took the shock of the charge without breaking ranks, hurled their own javelins, and then began to use their swords. . . . I gave the signal to the six cohorts which constituted my fourth line. They went forward immediately to the attack and fell upon Pompey's cavalry with such violence that not one of the enemy stood up to the charge. . . . It was at this moment that I ordered my third line to charge. . . . Pompey's men now found themselves attacked by an entirely fresh body of troops. . . . They were unable to resist; the entire army turned and fled. After seeing [this] rout [great defeat] . . . Pompey despaired also of the rest, left the battle line, and rode straight to his camp.[64]

After the battle Pompey fled to Egypt. The ruler there was a boy—Ptolemy XIII, a descendant of Alexander the Great's general of the same name. Pompey hoped that Ptolemy would give him refuge from Caesar. But Ptolemy's advisors warned him that helping Pompey would bring Caesar's wrath down on Egypt, so the young king had Pompey killed as his boat neared the shore. Plutarch recalled:

> As he rose from his seat in the boat, he was treacherously stabbed in the back. He, therefore, taking up his gown with both hands, drew it over his face, and neither saying nor doing anything unworthy of himself, only groaning a little, endured the wounds they gave him, and so ended his life.[65]

The Ides of March

Ptolemy had Pompey's head cut off and sent to Caesar, hoping this token would keep the Roman conqueror from coming to Egypt. But Caesar came anyway. He stayed in Egypt for a year, during which he became involved in a power struggle between Ptolemy and his sister Cleopatra. This reportedly beautiful and wily young girl won Caesar's favor, partly through seducing him. With the aid of Mark Antony, who arrived with extra troops, Caesar helped Cleopatra overcome her brother's forces and saw to it that she became Egypt's queen and sole ruler.

Eventually Caesar returned to Rome, where, in 46 B.C., he had himself made

After being smuggled inside bed linens into his chamber, Cleopatra greets Caesar for the first time.

Caesar's corpse lies at the base of Pompey's statue as the conspirators exit the Senate proclaiming "Liberty!"

The Fault Is in Ourselves, Not Our Stars

William Shakespeare wrote his great political tragedy Julius Caesar *in 1599. He based it largely on* Plutarch's Life of Caesar, *and also used as references the writings of the ancient historians Livy, Tacitus, Polybius, Appian, Suetonius, and Caesar himself. In the opening of the play the senator Cassius attempts to convince Brutus, another senator and Caesar's friend, that Caesar has become too ambitious and must be stopped. The following speech, although written sixteen centuries after the events depicted, likely captures the feelings and arguments of the real Cassius.*

"Why, man, he doth bestride the narrow world
Like a Colossus [giant statue], and we petty men
Walk under his huge legs and peep about
To find ourselves dishonorable graves.
Men at some time are masters of their fates.
The fault, dear Brutus, is not in our stars [destiny according to birth sign],
 But in ourselves, that we are underlings.
'Brutus' and 'Caesar.' What should be in that 'Caesar'?
Why should that name be sounded more than yours?
Write them together: yours is as fair a name.
Sound them: it doth become the mouth as well.
Weigh them: it is as heavy. Conjur [perform magic] with 'em:
'Brutus' will start [raise] a spirit as soon as 'Caesar.'
Now in the names of all the gods at once,
Upon what meat doth this our Caesar feed
That he is grown so great? Age, thou art shamed!
Rome, thou hast lost the breed of noble bloods!
When went there by an age since the great Flood
But it was famed with more than with one man?
When could they say [till now] that talked of Rome
That her wide walls encompassed but one man?
Now is it Rome indeed, and room enough,
When there is in it but one only man!
O you and I have heard our fathers say
There was a Brutus once [one of the republic's founders] that would have brooked [tolerated]
The eternal devil to keep his state in Rome
As easily as a king."

dictator for a ten-year period. Two years later, he changed this term to life. No longer did he attempt to hide his ambitions behind the trappings of republican government. Through the use of his military forces, he began to transform Rome into his own absolute monarchy. The Roman historian Appian wrote:

Slaves carry Caesar's body across the Roman Forum. According to the Roman historian Appian, Caesar sustained twenty-three knife wounds.

All kinds of honors were devised for his gratification . . . sacrifices, games, statues in all the temples and public places. . . . He was proclaimed the Father of his Country and chosen dictator for life and consul for ten years and his person was declared sacred. . . . It was decreed that he should transact business on a throne of ivory and gold . . . that each year the city should celebrate the days on which he had won his victories. . . . In honor of his birth the name of the month Quintilis was changed to July. Many temples were decreed [dedicated] to him as to a god.[66]

All of this insulted and angered most senators and many other Romans, who saw that their beloved republic was in extreme peril. Desperate to save the government, several senators conspired in a plot to kill Caesar. Their chance came on March 15, the "ides of March," 44 B.C. Caesar visited the Senate that day, and because he had become so arrogant that he had recently dismissed his bodyguards, he came alone. As he entered the Senate chamber, a group of conspirators, led by the senators Brutus and Cassius, suddenly attacked and stabbed him to death. Ironically, the dictator fell at the feet of a statue of Pompey, his rival. The conspirators then ran into the streets crying, "Liberty!" But their victory over Caesar proved empty, for though he was dead, other ambitious men were eager to take his place. Despite the high hopes of many on that fateful day, the republic was mortally wounded, and the turbulent and bloody events of the next few years would sound its final death knell.

8 Octavian Triumphant: The Fall of the Republic

Julius Caesar's sudden death left a power vacuum in Rome. The senators who had murdered the dictator assumed that the Senate would quickly regain its traditional powers and undo the damage to the republic that Caesar and other power generals had done. But this did not happen. To their surprise, the conspirators found little popular support for their violent act. This

(Left) Marcus Aemilius Lepidus and (right) Mark Antony, two members of the Second Triumvirate.

was partly because Caesar's two strongest allies, Mark Antony, now serving as consul, and Marcus Lepidus, a powerful general, were still in Rome. They enjoyed the support of both the army and a large number of citizens, rich and poor. Caesar had also left an heir, his eighteen-year-old grand-nephew Gaius Octavius, known as Octavian. The constantly shifting intrigues, alliances, and power struggles among these three men would keep Rome entangled in destructive civil strife for another fifteen years. Eventually, one of them would emerge from the fray and restore order, but under a system far different from the one that had guided Rome for centuries.

The Rise of Octavian

After Caesar's death Antony wasted no time in establishing his authority. Using the army to intimidate the senators, as Caesar had done, Antony kept the senators from repealing any of Caesar's laws. In addition, he made the senators approve several other laws that Caesar had only recently proposed. Then, on the day of Caesar's funeral, standing before a huge crowd that had come to see the dead leader's body, Antony delivered a stirring speech. Sixteen

Antony's funeral oration over Caesar's body. Shakespeare later gave Antony the words, "Here is himself, marr'd, as you see, with traitors."

centuries later the English playwright William Shakespeare would give Antony the immortal opening words, "Friends, Romans, countrymen, lend me your ears. I come to bury Caesar, not to praise him." The wily Antony not only ended up praising Caesar, but also revealed to the crowd the contents of Caesar's will. The dictator had left his private gardens as a public park and also granted a small sum of money to every Roman citizen. The rest of his fortune Caesar had left to Octavian, whom he had recently adopted as his son.

Antony went on to point out all the great deeds Caesar had accomplished for Rome and reminded the people that they had once proudly supported him. Wrote Plutarch:

> As he was ending his speech, he took the under-clothes of the dead, and held them up, showing them stains of blood and the holes of the many stabs, calling those that had done this act villains and bloody murderers. All of

which excited the people to such indignation, that they would not defer [delay] the funeral, but, making a pile of tables . . . set fire to it; and every one, taking a brand [burning stick], ran to the conspirators' houses to attack them.[67]

Fearing for their lives, the conspirators fled the city.

It now seemed that Antony was all-powerful in Rome. But his expectation of taking Caesar's place was short-lived. When Octavian arrived to collect his inheritance, Antony, who was handling Caesar's will, refused to hand over the money. Antony assumed that the rather sickly youth was weak and could easily be manipulated. But he had completely underestimated Octavian. The young man immediately raised a small army composed of Caesar's veterans and joined forces with Cicero, who wanted to keep Antony from becoming a dictator like Caesar. In 43 B.C. it was Antony who had to flee Rome.

With Antony out of the way, Octavian, now nineteen, demanded the office of consul. But Cicero and his fellow senators refused. They had only been using Octavian to get rid of Antony and had no intention of letting him hold such a powerful post. But they, too, had underestimated Octavian's abilities. He swiftly marched his army into Rome, and the surprised senators had no choice but to make him consul.

The Second Triumvirate

Octavian realized that the Senate would continue to oppose him and that to control it effectively he needed to expand his power base. So he wisely suggested to Antony that they settle their differences and unite. Jumping at this chance to regain power, Antony agreed, and, with Lepidus and Octavian, formed the Second Triumvirate in the winter of 43 B.C. According to Appian:

> Octavian and Antony composed their differences on a small, gradually sloping islet in the river Lavinius near the city of Mutina [in northern Italy]. Each had five legions of soldiers whom they stationed opposite each other. . . . Lepidus himself went before them, searched the island, and shook his military cloak as a signal to them to come. . . . There the three sat together in council, Octavian in the center because he was consul. They were in conference from morning till night for two days and came to these decisions . . . that a new magistracy [ruling body— the triumvirate, in this case] for quieting the civil dissensions [disagreements] should be created by law, which Lepidus,

Despite his youth, Octavian was a shrewd politician.

Antony, and Octavian should hold for five years . . . that a distribution of the provinces should be made, giving to Antony the whole of Gaul. . . . Spain was assigned to Lepidus, while Octavian was to have Africa, Sardinia, and Sicily.[68]

The triumvirs immediately launched a series of proscriptions against their enemies, just as Sulla had done years before. The first name Antony put on the list of condemned was Cicero, who symbolized the power and spirit of the republic the three men were attempting to control. Cicero was trying to escape to the seacoast when Antony's henchmen caught up with him. Recording the end of one of the republic's greatest patriots, Plutarch wrote:

> The assassins were come [to Cicero's house] with a band of soldiers, Herrenius, a centurion, and Popillius, a tribune. . . . Finding the doors shut, they

A Phantom Visit

According to stories and rumors passed around after the battle of Philippi, in which Brutus's army was defeated by that of Antony and Octavian, Brutus learned before the battle that he was doomed. The supernatural visitation described in Plutarch's Lives *was widely believed by the Romans and clearly illustrates how much stock the people of that time put in predetermined fate and evil omens. According to Plutarch, one night Brutus was lying awake in his tent when he received an unexpected visit:*

"He heard a noise at the door, and looking that way, by the light of his lamp, which was almost out, saw a terrible figure, like that of a man, but of unusual stature and severe countenance [appearance]. He [Brutus] was somewhat frightened at first, but seeing it neither did nor spoke anything to him, only stood silently by his bedside, he asked who it was. The spectre [ghost] answered him, 'Thy evil genius, Brutus, thou shalt see me at Philippi.' Brutus answered courageously, 'Well, I shall see you,' and immediately the appearance vanished. The night before the battle the same phantom appeared to him again, but spoke not a word. He presently understood his destiny [fated death] was at hand [near] and exposed himself to all the danger of the battle. Yet he did not die in the fight, but seeing his men defeated, got up to the top of a rock and fell upon his sword and thus met his death."

Brutus kills himself after the defeat of his republican forces at Philippi.

broke them open, and Cicero not appearing . . . it is stated that a [slave] . . . informed the tribune that the litter [Cicero's traveling couch carried by slaves] was on its way to the sea. . . . The tribune, taking a few [soldiers] with him, ran to the place where he [Cicero] was to come out. And Cicero, perceiving Herrenius . . . commanded his servants to set down the litter; and stroking his chin, as he used to do . . . he looked steadfastly upon his murderers, his person covered with dust, his beard and hair untrimmed, and his face worn with his troubles. So that the greatest part of those that stood by covered their faces while Herrenius slew him. And thus was he murdered, stretching forth his neck out of the litter, being now in his sixty-fourth year. Herrenius cut off his head, and, by Antony's command, his hands also.[69]

To remind all Romans that the republic was a thing of the past, Antony ordered Cicero's head and hands nailed to a platform in Rome's main square. Then, in full public view, Antony's wife Fulvia cruelly pierced the dead man's tongue with her dress pin.

Brutus, one of the republic's last champions. Shakespeare called him "the noblest Roman of them all."

The Triumvirate Begins to Crumble

But the triumvirs could not yet celebrate total victory. Though their main opponent was dead, forces loyal to the republic were ready to make one last stand against them. After fleeing Italy to Greece, Brutus and Cassius had managed to raise about eighty thousand loyal troops, and they awaited a showdown with the triumvirs. Antony and Octavian obliged them in the summer of 42 B.C. The armies met on the plain of Philippi in northern Greece and, as Appian told it, everyone involved knew that the republic was at stake.

> [The soldiers] did not now remember that they were fellow-citizens of their enemies, but hurled threats at each other as though they had been enemies by birth and descent, so much did the anger of the moment extinguish reason and nature in them. Both sides divined [realized] equally that this day and this battle would decide the fate of Rome completely; and so indeed it did.[70]

A Terrible Slaughter

The battle of Philippi, fought in 42 B.C. in Greece, decided once and for all whether the Roman Republic would survive or be swept aside by power-hungry men. Appian recorded the details of that battle in his Roman History.

"[The soldiers in the two armies] did not now remember that they were fellow-citizens of their enemies, but hurled threats at each other as though they had been enemies by birth and descent, so much did the anger of the moment extinguish reason and nature in them. Both sides divined [realized] equally that this day and this battle would decide the fate of Rome completely; and so indeed it did. The day was consumed in preparations till the ninth hour, when two eagles fell upon [attacked] each other and fought in the space between the armies, amid the profoundest silence. When the one on the side of Brutus took flight his enemies raised a great shout and battle was joined. The onset was superb and terrible. They had little need of arrows, stones or javelins, which are customary in war, for they did not resort to the usual maneuvers and tactics of battles, but, coming to close combat with naked swords, they slew and were slain, seeking to break each other's ranks. . . . The slaughter and the groans were terrible. The bodies of the fallen were carried back and others stepped into their places from the reserves. . . . Finally, the soldiers of Octavian . . . pushed back the enemy's line. . . . The latter were driven back step by step. . . . Presently their ranks broke and they retreated more rapidly. . . . These fled, some to the sea, and some through the river Zygactes to the mountains."

After hours of fierce and bloody fighting, Antony's forces won the day. Beaten and humiliated, Brutus and Cassius committed suicide by falling on their swords, and the last chance to restore the republic died with them.

Antony and Octavian proceeded to redivide the empire between themselves. They were powerful enough now to push aside Lepidus, whom they suspected of plotting against them. Antony agreed to reorganize the eastern provinces, while Octavian returned to Rome to provide land for the 170,000 troops under their command. Both men realized that the key to their power still lay in making the soldiers happy. Octavian found that there was little Italian public land available, so he baldly confiscated large tracts from innocent landowners. Many Romans were outraged, but with the government now powerless, there was nothing they could do.

In the following few years, an uneasy truce continued between Antony and Octavian. Neither man trusted the other, but they were content for the moment to maintain their alliance. During these years Antony fought a number of border wars in the eastern provinces, while Octavian cemented his powers in Italy and the western empire. Octavian won over many of Rome's disgruntled citizens by pretending to support the old rule of law. He let the Senate and other arms of government function in a seemingly normal fashion, but it was he who actually made the vital decisions. The republic now existed in name only. In 36 B.C. Octavian further increased his power when Lepidus boldly challenged him for control of Sicily. A battle appeared imminent, but at the last minute Lepidus's troops deserted him and joined Octavian. Lepidus lost his titles and power and remained under house arrest until his death twenty-four years later.

Antony Bewitched

With Octavian the supreme power in the west and Antony in charge of the east, a clash between the two ambitious men was inevitable. To justify the civil war he desired with Antony, Octavian launched a bitter smear campaign against his rival. Octavian charged Antony of shirking his duties and wavering in his allegiance to Rome as a result of being led astray by Egypt's queen, Cleopatra. To some degree, this charge was true. Antony had first met Cleopatra in 41 B.C., when she paid him a visit in Cilicia in southern Asia Minor. According to Plutarch:

> She came sailing up the river in a barge with gilded [gold-covered] stern and outspread sails of purple, while oars of silver beat time to the music of flutes and fifes and harps. She herself lay under a canopy of cloth of gold, dressed as Venus in a picture, and beautiful young boys . . . stood on each side to fan her. Her maids were dressed like sea-nymphs [goddesses]. . . . The perfumes diffused themselves [spread] from the vessel to the shore, which was covered with multitudes, part running out of the city to see the sight. On her arrival, Antony set to invite her to supper. She thought it fitter that he should come to her. . . . The enchanting queen captivated him. Her beauty joined with the charm of her conversation, and . . . was bewitching.[71]

The two became notorious lovers, and in the years that followed Antony spent much of his time in Egypt visiting Cleopatra. He frequently adopted Egyptian habits and dress and often did neglect his duties. Octavian took full advantage of the situation, convincing the Roman people that Cleopatra wanted to be queen of Rome and that Antony planned to seize the empire for her. Though these stories were exaggerated, some evidence suggests that Cleopatra did intend to use Antony to further her own ambitions. In any case, the propaganda swayed public opinion in Rome heavily against Antony and Cleopatra. In the fall of 33 B.C. Octavian finally felt the time was right and declared war on Antony. Once more, Roman would be forced to fight Roman.

Defeat and Suicide

The new civil war consisted largely of a single battle. Antony and Cleopatra managed to raise ninety thousand troops and five hundred ships, with which they intended to invade Italy. These forces spent the winter of 32–31 B.C. in southern Greece. In the spring of 31 B.C. Octavian, aided by a skilled general named Agrippa, approached Greece with land and sea forces slightly smaller than Antony's. In the bay of Actium on the western coast of Greece, the fleets met in a great battle in which many ships burned and thousands on both sides lost their lives. The Roman historian Dio Cassius wrote:

> Some sailors perished by the smoke before the flames could reach them; others were cooked in their armor, which

Octavian inspects the body of Antony, who had been both his ally and enemy.

Agrippa, Octavian's able military advisor, was largely responsible for the Roman victory at Actium.

became red hot; others were roasted in their vessels as though in ovens. Many leaped into the sea; of these, some were mangled by sea monsters [sharks], some were shot by arrows, some were drowned.[72]

At the height of the battle, for reasons unknown, Cleopatra suddenly fled the scene. Soon afterward, to the astonishment of all involved, Antony abandoned his own forces and joined her. Most of his remaining ships then surrendered to Octavian, as did his land troops.

Antony and Cleopatra returned to Egypt, where they hoped to make a final stand. But after Octavian landed there, Antony's few remaining troops deserted him. Disgraced and ruined, Antony committed suicide. Cleopatra soon followed

A Battle Lost over the Love of a Woman

Octavian's defeat of Antony and Cleopatra ensured his subsequent rise to power as the first Roman emperor. The battle of Actium was one of the largest and most decisive sea battles ever fought. In Life of Antony, *Plutarch describes the beginning of the battle and Cleopatra's and Antony's flight:*

"Antony in a small boat went from one ship to another, encouraging his soldiers. . . . After examining . . . his fleet, [Caesar, or Octavian] went in a boat to the right wing, and looked with much admiration at the enemy lying perfectly still in the straits, in all appearance as if they had been at anchor. . . . But about noon a breeze sprang up from the sea, and Antony's men . . . began to advance the left squadron [group of ships]. When they were engaged, there was no charging or striking of one ship by another, because Antony's, by reason of their great bulk, were incapable of the great rapidity required to make the [oar] stroke effectual, and on the other side, Caesar's [ships] dared not charge head to head on Antony's, which were all armed with solid masses and spikes of brass. . . . The engagement resembled . . . the attack and defense of a fortified place; for there were always three or four vessels of Caesar's [around] one of Antony's, pressing them with spears, javelins, poles, and several inventions of fire, which they flung among them, Antony's men using catapults also, to pour down missiles from wooden towers. . . . But the fortune of the day was still undecided, and the battle equal, when on a sudden Cleopatra's sixty ships were seen hoisting sail and making out to sea in full flight, right through the ships that were engaged. . . . Here it was that Antony showed to all the world that he was no longer actuated [motivated] by the thoughts and motives of a commander or a man, or indeed by his own judgment at all, and what was once said as a jest, that the soul of a lover lives in someone else's body, he proved to be a serious truth. For, as if he had been born part of her, and must move with her wheresoever she went . . . he abandoned all that were fighting and spending their lives for him, and put himself aboard a galley of five banks of oars, to follow her that had so well begun his ruin and would hereafter accomplish it."

In this semi-fanciful painting, Octavian stands at Cleopatra's deathbed.
In reality, he did not witness her suicide.

him, allowing herself to be bitten by poisonous snakes called asps. Wrote the Roman poet Horace:

> She nerved herself unmoved to look
>   Upon her wrecked domains;
> And gripped the asps and deeply took
>   Their venom in her veins:
>
> No brutal ships, no triumph high,
>   With her should work their will;
> Flushed with her dark resolve to die,
>   Unqueened, but queenly still.[73]

From Octavian to Augustus

At the age of thirty-two Octavian had triumphed over all adversaries and emerged as the sole power in Rome and its vast empire. In 29 B.C. he returned to Rome, where he enjoyed a lavish three-day victory celebration. Soon afterward he imposed a new government on Rome. On the surface it appeared similar to the old system. There were still the Senate, the courts, the assemblies, and various public officials, and Octavian allowed these to carry on most of the normal business of state.

But, in reality, the republic no longer existed, because the government was no longer in the hands of the people. Octavian still controlled the armies. Though he wisely did not use his military power openly to threaten the government, as his predecessors had, he was in a very real sense a military dictator, and everyone knew it. He also exercised his own direct rule over Egypt, as well as Gaul and many other provinces, thus limiting the administrative

The Bite of the Asp

According to Plutarch in Life of Antony, *once she had made up her mind to commit suicide, Cleopatra carefully searched for a poison that would not cause her too much pain:*

"Cleopatra was busied in making a collection of all varieties of poisonous drugs, and, in order to see which of them were the least painful in the operation, she had them tried upon prisoners condemned to die. But, finding that the quick poisons always worked with sharp pains, and that the less painful were slow, she next tried venomous animals, and watching with her own eyes whilst they were applied, one creature to the body of another. This was her daily practice, and she pretty well satisfied herself that nothing was comparable to the bite of the asp [a snake], which, without convulsion or groaning, brought on a heavy drowsiness and lethargy [slowness], with a gentle sweat on the face, the senses being stupified [dulled] by degrees; the patient, in appearance, being sensible of no pain, but rather troubled to be disturbed or awakened like those that are in a profound [deep] natural sleep."

Cleopatra surveys the battle of Actium from the deck of one of the sixty ships she commanded in the fight.

A statue of Octavian after he assumed the title of Augustus, "the exalted one."

In these and other ways, Octavian assumed dictatorial powers while wisely avoiding titles like dictator or king, which he realized the Roman people had come to despise and mistrust. He chose instead to project the benevolent image of savior and protector of the people. In 27 B.C., he took the title of Imperator Caesar Augustus, "The Great Victor and Ruler." (The word *emperor* later developed from the word *imperator.*) But Octavian himself never used the title of emperor, preferring to be called either Augustus or *princeps,* meaning "first citizen." Whatever he chose to call himself at the time, he was in fact the first in a long line of Roman emperors. Beginning with his reign, Rome and its provinces became known as the Roman Empire.

Augustus enjoyed a long, successful, and peaceful reign. After more than a century of bloodshed, power struggles, and civil strife, the Roman people were thankful for the order and stability he brought. In time, most people remembered the days of the republic as a time of troubles and chaos and the idea of restoring it steadily died out. Though the system that had brought Rome power and prestige for five hundred years was gone, Rome's days of glory were not over. The Romans were embarking on a new era of accomplishments that would profoundly affect the many lands and peoples they would encounter and thereby help to shape the next two thousand years of world history.

powers of the government mainly to Italy. In addition, Octavian skillfully maneuvered the Senate into granting him a number of important powers. He held authority similar to that of a consul or tribune, so he could both propose and veto any law or policy he desired. He also reserved the rights to make war or peace without having to consult the Senate, to call meetings of that body, and to nominate many of the candidates for office voted on in the assemblies.

Notes

Introduction: A Genius for the Practical

1. Edith Hamilton, *The Roman Way to Western Civilization.* New York: New American Library, 1960.
2. Sallust, *The War with Catiline,* quoted in Stringfellow Barr, *The Mask of Jove: A History of Graeco-Roman Civilization from the Death of Alexander to the Death of Constantine.* Philadelphia: J. B. Lippincott, 1966.
3. Hamilton, *The Roman Way.*

Chapter 1: Village on the Tiber: Rome Is Established

4. Livy, *History of Rome,* trans. W. M. Roberts, in Dorothy Mills, *The Book of the Ancient Romans.* New York: G. P. Putnam's Sons, 1927.
5. Plutarch, *Life of Romulus,* in *Lives of the Noble Grecians and Romans,* trans. John Dryden. New York: Random House, 1932.
6. Livy, *History of Rome.*
7. Livy, *History of Rome.*
8. Anthony Marks and Graham Tingay, *The Romans.* London: Usborne Publishing, 1990.
9. Quoted in Donald R. Dudley, *The Civilization of Rome.* New York: New American Library, 1960.
10. Quoted in Chester G. Starr, *The Ancient Romans.* New York: Oxford University Press, 1971.
11. Quoted in Starr, *The Ancient Romans.*
12. Arthur E. R. Boak, *A History of Rome to 565 A.D.* New York: Macmillan, 1943.

13. Quoted in Mills, *The Book of the Ancient Romans.*
14. Plutarch, *Lives.*
15. James Henry Breasted, *Ancient Times: A History of the Early World.* Boston: Ginn, 1944.

Chapter 2: Roman Republic: The Unification of Italy

16. Livy, *History of Rome.*
17. Starr, *The Ancient Romans.*
18. Livy, *History of Rome.*
19. Livy, *History of Rome.*
20. Paul J. Alexander, ed., *The Ancient World: to 300 A.D.* New York: Macmillan, 1963.
21. Quoted in Dudley, *The Civilization of Rome.*
22. Quoted in Mills, *The Book of the Ancient Romans.*
23. Livy, *History of Rome.*
24. Quoted in Starr, *The Ancient Romans.*

Chapter 3: Punic Wars: Rome and Carthage Battle for Supremacy

25. Plutarch, *Life of Pyrrhus,* in *Lives.*
26. Frank R. Cowell, *Cicero and the Roman Republic.* Baltimore: Penguin, 1967.
27. Breasted, *Ancient Times.*
28. Polybius, *Histories,* quoted in Will Durant, *Caesar and Christ: A History of Roman Civilization and of Christianity from Their Beginnings to A.D. 325.* New York: Simon and Schuster, 1944.
29. Polybius, *Histories,* in *The Ancient World: to 300 A.D.*

30. Cornelius Nepos, *Life of Hannibal*, quoted in Mills, *The Book of the Ancient Romans*.
31. Livy, *History of Rome*.
32. Starr, *The Ancient Romans*.
33. Livy, *History of Rome*.

Chapter 4: Conquest and Expansion: The Mediterranean Becomes a Roman Lake

34. Livy, *History of Rome*.
35. Polybius, *Histories*, in *The Ancient World: to 300* A.D.
36. Juvenal, *Satires*, quoted in Lionel Casson, *Daily Life in Ancient Rome*. New York: American Heritage Publishing, 1975.
37. Juvenal, *Satires*.
38. Livy, *History of Rome*.
39. Martial, quoted in Casson, *Daily Life in Ancient Rome*.
40. Cato, quoted in Livy, *History of Rome*.
41. Plautus, *The Merchant*, quoted in Hamilton, *The Roman Way*.
42. Polybius, *Histories*, in Mills, *The Book of the Ancient Romans*.

Chapter 5: Troubles of the Mighty: The Struggle to Maintain Order

43. Plutarch, *Life of Tiberius Gracchus*, in *Lives*.
44. Plutarch, *Life of Tiberius Gracchus*, in *Lives*.
45. Plutarch, *Life of Gaius Gracchus*, in *Lives*.
46. Plutarch, *Life of Gaius Marius*, in *Lives*.
47. Polybius, *Histories*.
48. Polybius, *Histories*.
49. Plutarch, *Life of Sulla*, in *Lives*.
50. Plutarch, *Life of Sulla*, in *Lives*.

Chapter 6: Fighting Slaves and Pirates: Strongmen Vie for Power

51. Plutarch, *Life of Crassus*, in *Lives*.
52. Durant, *Caesar and Christ*.
53. Cowell, *Cicero and the Roman Republic*.
54. Plutarch, *Life of Crassus*, in *Lives*.
55. Plutarch, *Life of Pompey*, in *Lives*.
56. Starr, *The Ancient Romans*.
57. Plutarch, *Life of Pompey*, in *Lives*.

Chapter 7: Caesar's Exploits: The Republic in Peril

58. Cicero, quoted in R. H. Barrow, *The Romans*. Baltimore: Penguin, 1949.
59. Cicero, quoted in Barrow, *The Romans*.
60. Cicero, quoted in Barrow, *The Romans*.
61. Julius Caesar, *Commentaries on the Gallic Wars*, published as *War Commentaries of Caesar*, trans. Rex Warner. New York: New American Library, 1960.
62. Suetonius, *Julius Caesar*, quoted in Mills, *The Book of the Ancient Romans*.
63. Plutarch, *Life of Caesar*, in *Lives*.
64. Julius Caesar, *Commentaries*.
65. Plutarch, *Life of Pompey*, in *Lives*.
66. Appian, *Roman History*, quoted in Mills, *The Book of the Ancient Romans*.

Chapter 8: Octavian Triumphant: The Fall of the Republic

67. Plutarch, *Life of Antony*, in *Lives*.
68. Appian, *Roman History*.
69. Plutarch, *Life of Cicero*, in *Lives*.
70. Appian, *Roman History*.
71. Plutarch, *Life of Antony*, in *Lives*.
72. Dio Cassius, *History*, quoted in Durant, *Caesar and Christ*.
73. Horace, *Odes*, quoted in Mills, *The Book of the Ancient Romans*.

For Further Reading

Ian Andrews, *Pompeii*. Cambridge, England: Cambridge University Press, 1978. An easy-to-read, colorfully illustrated synopsis of the eruption of Mount Vesuvius, destruction of Pompeii, and the facts learned by archaeologists from excavating that buried city.

Lionel Casson, *Daily Life in Ancient Rome*. New York: American Heritage Publishing, 1975. A fascinating presentation of how the Romans lived: their homes, streets, entertainments, eating habits, theaters, religion, slaves, marriage customs, government, tombstone epitaphs, and much more.

Ann Kramer and Lindy Newton, editors, *Quest for the Past: Amazing Answers to the Riddles of History*. Pleasantville, NY: Reader's Digest Association, 1984. Contains several well researched and plainly written articles about ancient Rome, including farming and slaves, Hannibal's elephants, Roman travelers, and the religious cults of Bacchus.

Anthony Marks and Graham Tingay, *The Romans*. London: Usborne Publishing, 1990. Beautifully illustrated summary of Roman history and life, written for basic readers.

Chester G. Starr, *The Ancient Romans*. New York: Oxford University Press, 1971. General survey of Roman history with several interesting sidebars on such subjects as the Etruscans, Roman law, and the Roman army. Also contains many primary source quotes by ancient Roman and Greek writers.

Author's Note: I also strongly recommend the following films about the Roman Republic for their accuracy, dramatic impact, or both. All are available on videotape:

Caesar and Cleopatra (1946) with Vivian Leigh, Claude Rains, and Stewart Granger, directed by Gabriel Pascal. A beautifully photographed and well acted version of the play by George Bernard Shaw about the relationship of the title characters. Not completely accurate but delightfully entertaining.

Cleopatra (1963) with Elizabeth Taylor, Richard Burton, and Rex Harrison, directed by Joseph L. Mankiewicz. Overlong but visually stunning depiction of the affairs Cleopatra had with Julius Caesar and Mark Antony. Contains authentic sets and costumes, an excellent performance by Rex Harrison as Caesar, and incredibly spectacular reproductions of Cleopatra's parade into Rome and the sea battle of Actium.

Julius Caesar (1953) with Marlon Brando, James Mason, and John Gielgud, directed by Joseph L. Mankiewicz. Extremely well acted and dramatic version of Shakespeare's play about the last days of Caesar. The scenes between Mason as Brutus and Gielgud as Cassius are especially riveting.

Julius Caesar (1970) with Charlton Heston, Jason Robards, and John Gielgud, directed by Stuart Burge. A visually colorful version of the play, marred somewhat by Robard's monotone portrayal of Brutus. Gielgud plays Caesar in this one. Not as good as the earlier version but still worthwhile.

Spartacus (1960) with Kirk Douglas, Laurence Olivier, and Jean Simmons, directed by Stanley Kubrick. A colorful, exciting, and magnificently filmed epic about the slave who challenged Rome. Contains some fictional characters and situations but for the most part is remarkably factual. The authentic sets, costumes, weapons, and other details give an amazingly true picture of Roman life in the first century B.C.

Works Consulted

Paul J. Alexander, ed., *The Ancient World: to 300 A.D.* New York: Macmillan, 1963. A diverse collection of excerpts from ancient Greek and Roman works.

Appian, *History of Rome,* translated by Horace White. Cambridge, MA: Harvard University Press, 1961. Invaluable primary source describing in great detail the late republic, the Civil Wars, and the exploits of powerful men like Julius Caesar.

Stringfellow Barr, *The Mask of Jove: A History of Graeco-Roman Civilization from the Death of Alexander to the Death of Constantine.* Philadelphia: J. B. Lippincott, 1966. Long, well researched account of classical civilization. Contains a number of long primary source quotes. Difficult reading.

R. H. Barrow, *The Romans.* Baltimore: Penguin, 1949. Short but well written summary of both the Roman Republic and the Roman Empire.

Arthur E. R. Boak, *A History of Rome to 565 A.D.* New York: Macmillan, 1943. A detailed account of Roman history that pays special attention to political developments and intrigues. Advanced reading.

James Henry Breasted, *Ancient Times: A History of the Early World.* Boston: Ginn, 1944. One of the best general sources on ancient civilizations, extremely well researched, organized, and clearly written. Contains over 200 pages on Rome alone.

Julius Caesar, *Commentaries on the Gallic Wars,* published as *War Commentaries of Caesar,* translated by Rex Warner. New York: New American Library, 1960. Caesar's journal of his conquests of Gaul and Britain, as well as of the civil wars that wracked the republic. Reveals much about Roman politics, army life, battles, and also the lands and peoples of Europe at that time.

Frank R. Cowell, *Cicero and the Roman Republic.* Baltimore: Penguin, 1967. Detailed, interesting analysis of the Roman Republic, with plenty of useful and revealing statistics. Advanced reading.

Donald R. Dudley, *The Civilization of Rome.* New York: New American Library, 1960. Well written Roman history, with emphasis on cultural aspects.

Donald R. Dudley, *The Romans: 850 B.C.-A.D. 337.* New York: Alfred A. Knopf, 1970. Good general history of Rome.

J. Wight Duff, *A Literary History of Rome.* New York: Barnes and Noble, 1960. Lists and analyzes the important Roman writers and their works. A valuable reference book for those interested in Latin works. Advanced reading.

Will Durant, *Caesar and Christ: A History of Roman Civilization and of Christianity from Their Beginnings to A.D. 325.* New York: Simon and Schuster, 1944. Immense and brilliantly researched and organized summary of Roman civilization. Difficult reading.

Michael Grant, *The Founders of the Western World: A History of Greece and Rome.* New York: Charles Scribner's Sons, 1991. A general summary of Greek and Roman history. Advanced reading.

Michael Grant, *The World of Rome.* New York: New American Library, 1960. A fascinating view of Roman culture, including chapters with themes like "Subjects and Slaves," "Fate and the Stars," and "The Great Latin Writers." Contains plenty of primary source quotes revealing much about Roman life.

Kevin Guinagh and Alfred Paul Dorjahn, eds., *Latin Literature in Translation*. New York: Longman's, Green, 1952. Good selection of Roman writings, including those of Plautus, Terence, Caesar, Cato, Cicero, Sallust, Virgil, Horace, and many others. Advanced reading.

Edith Hamilton, *The Roman Way to Western Civilization*. New York: W. W. Norton, 1932, reprinted by New American Library, 1960. One of Hamilton's three timeless, classic, and beautifully written studies of the foundations of western culture, the others being *The Greek Way* and *Mythology*.

W. G. Hardy, *The Greek and Roman World*. Cambridge, MA: Schenkman Publishing, 1960. A brief but interesting overview of classical civilization.

Harold Whetstone Johnston, *The Private Life of the Romans*. New York: Cooper Square Publishers, 1973. Detailed study of everyday Roman life and customs, including chapters on the family, the role of women, food and meals, sources of income and means of living, funeral ceremonies, and others. Advanced reading.

Dorothy Mills, *The Book of the Ancient Romans*. New York: G. P. Putnam's Sons, 1927. Well researched summary of ancient Roman culture, supported by many long, fascinating primary source quotes.

Plutarch, *Lives of the Noble Grecians and Romans,* translated by John Dryden. New York: Random House, 1932. A complete, 1,296-page collection of the historian's biographical sketches of the fifty leading men in classical times. Most of the sources Plutarch used are gone, so this work preserves much knowledge that would otherwise be lost. Advanced reading.

Index

Picture Credits

About the Author

Don Nardo is an award-winning writer, composer, and filmmaker. His writing credits include short stories, articles, and more than forty-five books, including *Lasers, Gravity, Germs, The War of 1812, Medical Diagnosis, Eating Disorders, Charles Darwin, H. G. Wells, Thomas Jefferson,* and *Ancient Greece,* as well as *Cleopatra* and the companion volume to this book, *The Roman Empire.* Mr. Nardo has also written an episode for ABC's "Spenser: For Hire" and numerous screenplays. He lives with his wife, Christine, on Cape Cod, Massachusetts.